VORDAK
THE INCOMPREHENSIBLE

HOW TO GROW UP AND
RULE THE WORLD

EGMONT

EGMONT

We bring stories to life

First published by Egmont USA 2010
443 Park Avenue South, Suite 806, New York, NY 10016
First published in the UK by Egmont UK Ltd
239 Kensington High Street, London W8 6SA

Copyright © Scott Seegert, 2010
Illustrations by John Martin
All rights reserved

ISBN 978 1 4052 5204 1

10 9 8 7 6 5 4 3 2

www.egmont.co.uk
www.vordak.com

A CIP catalogue record for this title is available from the British Library

Printed and bound in Great Britain by CPI Books (Cox and Wyman)

Mixed Sources
Product group from well-managed
forests and other controlled sources
www.fsc.org Cert no. TT-COC-002332
© 1996 Forest Stewardship Council

Egmont is passionate about helping to preserve the world's remaining ancient forests.
We only use paper from legal and sustainable forest sources, so we know where every
single tree comes from that goes into every paper that makes up every book.

This book is made from paper certified by the Forestry Stewardship Council (FSC),
an organisation dedicated to promoting responsible management of forest resources.
For more information on the FSC, please visit **www.fsc.org**. To learn more about
Egmont's sustainable paper policy, please visit **www.egmont.co.uk/ethical**.

DEDICATION

To me, without whom not a single one of my glorious accomplishments would have been possible.

ACKNOWLEDGMENTS

I would like to commend my agent, Dan Lazar, my editor, Regina Griffin, and all the fine professionals at Egmont USA and Writers House for their wonderful contributions to this project. Unfortunately, I can't. A herd of bison would have been more helpful.

CONDOLENCES

I would like to take this opportunity to offer my sincere condolences to any other authors who have the misfortune to be releasing a book this year. As you are well aware, there is only so much attention to go around, and my book will rightfully be receiving the lion's share of it. Just so we are clear on this, I don't want to hear any whining.

Vordak

Contents

GLORIOUS ME!

Greetings, inferior one. I am Vordak the Incomprehensible. Who you are doesn't matter. What *does* matter is my dastardly decision to add the world of book publishing to my growing list of conquests. Without even trying very hard, I have created a book of such unbelievable brilliance that it dwarfs all other literature preceding it throughout the course of human history. The wisdom contained within these pages is of such humongousness that it offers even a piddling piece of pond scum such as yourself the opportunity to **ONE DAY GROW UP AND RULE THE WORLD! MUAHAHAHAHA!!!**

All right, hold on . . . Give me a second, here. The level of blowharded-ness I unleashed in that opening paragraph has left me a bit winded. No less evil, mind you, but winded. That's right—I'm evil. *Extremely* evil. Evil is who and what I am.

And as you can see from my awe-inspiring costume, I make no attempts to hide my evilosity from the world at large. I am tremendously proud of my heartless nature, and if you have any hopes of eventually becoming planetary dictator, you, too, will need to embrace your inner evil. I'm not talking "break your mother's favorite ceramic egg and blame it on your little brother" evil. I'm talking "willing to pull the moon into a collision course with the Earth by means of a powerful, nuclear-powered tractor beam in order to get your way" evil. I'm talking incredibly evil. Worse than your orthodontist.

I have decided to share a portion of my never-ending knowledge with those of you who prove to have "what it takes," which in this case happens to be £5.99. I realize that seems like quite a bit of money for a book, but when you consider the payoff is possession of all the wealth of human civilization, it's got to be worth £12.99 easy. Within these pages you'll find instructions, advice, charts, and illustrations, all of which were carefully crafted for the specific purpose of making the book thicker. I "auditioned" seventeen illustrators before finding one who could meet deadlines while generating artwork I deemed acceptable to include in the book.

I would have done it myself, but I did not want the magnificence of my artistic talent distracting readers from the text.

You will also be treated to my mind-numbing Commandments of Incomprehensibility, which appear periodically throughout the text. They highlight thoughts and ideas that contain especially high levels of wisdom—even for me. For example:

FIRST COMMANDMENT OF INCOMPREHENSIBILITY

Protect this book with your life. It is more valuable than the rest of your possessions combined. In fact, it is probably more valuable than your life, particularly if it's a signed copy.

I demand that tremendous care be taken while reading my masterpiece. Wear only gloves made from the finest acid-free Ethiopian ibex hair when handling the book. No other clothing—just the gloves. And remember to store the book in a dark, low-humidity, smoke-free environment, preferably deep space.

Copies of my book may be exhibited in your home using the temperature-controlled V-731 Priceless Object Display Vault.

To ensure that only magnificent copies are circulating across the globe, this book has been equipped with a microscopic self-destruct mechanism that will be triggered automatically in the event that so much as one page endures the slightest mistreatment, instantly vaporizing both the book and its reader (see the Fourth Commandment of Incomprehensibility, p. 22).

QUESTIONS

Part of what makes me "Incomprehensible" is my ability to predict the thoughts of those less intelligent than myself, which is pretty much everyone else on the planet, including you. And right now, I sense that you have a few questions, so I'll just go ahead and ask them for you, to prevent your measly little brain from overheating.

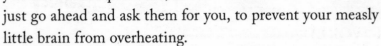

"What if I'm only looking to rule a portion of the world, like say Turkmenistan or Disney World?"

Then put this book back on the shelf immediately. Actually, pay for it first and then put it back on the shelf. Your lack of ambition quite frankly appalls me, and I refuse to allow your lazy little fingertips to contaminate these pages for one moment longer. There are plenty of other books that should suit your "needs" rather nicely.

"Why do I have to be evil in order to rule the world?"

Think of the nicest, most non-evil person you know. Perhaps your grandmother. Or a teacher. Or the postman. Now ask yourself: Does this person **RULE THE WORLD?** I didn't think so. Therefore it becomes obvious* that one must be evil in order to **RULE THE WORLD!**

* WHEN I STATE THAT SOMETHING IS "OBVIOUS", I MEAN, OF COURSE, THAT IT IS OBVIOUS TO ME. YOU, ON THE OTHER HAND, WILL SIMPLY HAVE TO TAKE MY WORD FOR IT.

You can take my Evil Aptitude Exam, that's how. Simply choose the response that best describes what you would do in each of the situations presented. You have thirty seconds to complete the exam. You may begin . . . *now!*

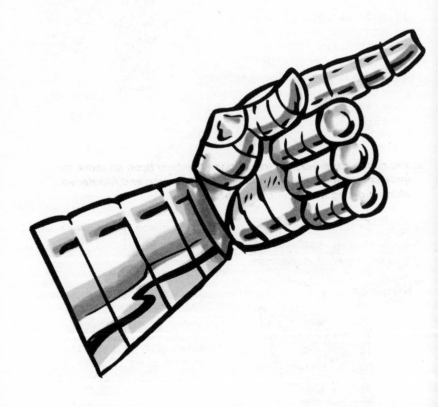

VORDAK THE INCOMPREHENSIBLE'S
Evil Aptitude Exam

1. While riding your bike you notice a woman attempting to transport a house plant across a busy intersection. Disregarding your own safety, you immediately:

a) Hop off your bike and offer to help her across the street.

b) Sell overpriced popcorn and soda to captivated bystanders.

c) Use your handlebar-mounted light-bending ray to make her virtually invisible to oncoming traffic.

2. You spot a cat stuck in a tree. It has obviously been up there for quite some time and appears to be cold, hungry, and frightened. Without giving it a second thought, you:

a) Run to the fire department to get help.

b) Walk very slowly to the fire department to get help.

c) Tap into your advanced knowledge of genetic engineering to create a tree-climbing pit bull.

3. You learn that your school's new foreign exchange student, who is from Iceland and speaks very little English, has a crush on a girl in his math class. You see this as the perfect opportunity to:

a) Help him out by introducing the two of them.

b) Inform him that the English translation of the Icelandic phrase "We're in the next class together—may I carry your books?" is "Due to problematic diarrhea, I am already into my seventh pair of underwear this morning."

c) Use your handlebar-mounted light-bending ray to give him the appearance of a cat when in the vicinity of tree-climbing pit bulls.

4. After discovering a $100 bill lying on the sidewalk, you decide to:

a) Do everything within your power to find the rightful owner in order to return the money.

b) Do everything within your power to find the rightful owner in order to wave the bill in his or her face and point out that you are the keeper while they, alas, are the weeper.

c) Use it as a down payment on a missile silo.

5. Upon entering your school's cafeteria, you spot Milton Schleppson, the smallest, feeblest kid in the entire school, lying facedown on the floor, covered with what appears to be a mixture of split pea soup and apple sauce, while a large gathering of his fellow students point and laugh hysterically. You immediately rush to Milton's side in order to:

a) Help him to his feet.

b) Use your cell phone camera to record a video for uploading on to YouTube.

c) Apply a nuclear wedgie, in which the victim's underwear is stretched to such an extent it may now be worn comfortably by a sumo wrestler.

それも終わったか？*

"Are you through with those?"

STOP! Your time is up. Put your pencil down and proceed immediately to the scoring key.

Scoring Key:

Award yourself 1 point for every "a" answer, 2 points for every "b," and 3 points for every "c."

Extra credit
Add 1 point if you didn't really stop when you were instructed to.
Add 1 point if you attempted to copy off someone else's exam, even if that person is stupid.
Add 1 point if you used the time you had left over to sketch plans for a fully functional submarine-mounted tectonic-plate-destabilization beam generator in the margin.

Score

(0–7) I'm sorry to say you will probably never RULE THE WORLD! And even if by some miracle you do, you'll just waste all of your power on things like promoting world peace and improving the environment and . . . snuggling. I'm familiar with your type. I suggest you read Chapter 1: Bringing Out the Evil seven or eight times and then try retaking the exam. It wouldn't hurt to whack somebody in the knees every now and again, either.

(8–14) You're on the right track. Although you can't yet be considered truly evil, you are quite mean—loathsome, even—which is a good start. And you have plenty of time to get worse. Your current level of eviltude will most likely allow you to rise only as high as your school's student council, but you will no doubt inflict some serious chaos once there. Read Chapter 1 carefully and you should be well on your way to ever-increasing levels of maliciousness.

(15+) Your heart beats cold and black. Your pores ooze evil. Well, they ooze sweat, but it's definitely an evil sweat. And not just because it smells bad, either. With a little training, your sweat would be fully capable of oppressing a small island nation all by itself. And you're probably a Yankees fan. You can skip Chapter 1 altogether.

"Why are you so willing to divulge your evil secrets?"

To an undeserving whelp such as yourself? Well, I'm not as young as I used to be. My neck grows weary of supporting my awe-inspiring Helmet of Disconcertment, and I simply no longer possess the energy required to conquer the planet myself. So I've decided to go this route.

Now, if you will simply apply your signature to the following standard evil promise of blah-da-blah-da-blah, which would be a foolish waste of your time to read over carefully, we'll be free to proceed with this introduction:

STANDARD EVIL PROMISE OF EMPLOYMENT AGREEMENT

(which would be a foolish waste of your time to read over carefully)

I, _____ (*aka* _____),

YOUR LEGAL NAME   YOUR EVIL WORLD RULER NAME
SEE PAGES 48–52

in the event that my mastery of the incomparable wisdom contained within these pages leads to my becoming **EVIL RULER OF THE WORLD (MUAHAHAHAHA!!)**, do hereby agree to appoint Vordak the Incomprehensible to the position of Second in Command (otherwise known as "Number 2", "Right-Hand Man", "Second Banana", "Mr. Fancy Pants") inclusive of all rights and privileges to which said position is entitled, including a private office, full health benefits, a reserved parking space, and the **IMMEDIATE ASCENSION** to the position of **EVIL RULER OF THE WORLD (MUAHAHAHAHA!!)** in the event that I were to die suddenly in some totally unexpected manner such as being poisoned, having my brake lines cut, being pushed down a well, having plutonium injected into my bloodstream, being encased in cement and dropped into the Mariana Trench, being dismembered by a previously obedient domestic robot, having my bodily fluids slowly and painfully drained by a giant, mutated spider while I lay paralyzed in bed, or anything else he might think of.

When completed, mail to:
Vordak the Incomprehensible
c/o Walter and Irene the Incomprehensible
21 East Bournier Street
Trenton, NJ 55555

No, but I *have* come agonizingly close on a number of occasions only to be thwarted by ~~my mistakes my occasional lapses in judgment~~ circumstances that were completely beyond my control—which reminds me:

SECOND COMMANDMENT OF INCOMPREHENSIBILITY

Never believe Commander Virtue when he assures you there is no need to confiscate his utility belt because there is nothing in there that he can use to escape from your latest diabolically clever yet extremely slow-acting death trap.

Apparently, honesty is not one of his virtues.

Nothing would please me more—not because you requested it, but because I believe there exists no more worthy a subject of discussion anywhere in the universe. My experience was actually a pretty standard one as far as evil childhoods go.

My father, Walter the Incomprehensible, struggled valiantly right up until his retirement to gain unquestioned dominion over the Earth. Alas, he rose only as high as mayor of Gomersborough, a small town in central Wisconsin. But he was a very evil small-town mayor, and the work ethic and dedication he displayed in his repeated attempts to conquer neighboring towns and villages helped shape me as I was growing up. To this day, I still have fond memories of the time our family spent together around the dinner table:

Mom: "And how was your day, Walter?"

Dad: "Excellent! Not only did the Department of Public Works complete the installation of my satellite-mounted XZ7000 Remote Laser Cannon, but I was also able to divert a delivery of chicken feed originally bound for Starksville to Norrin City—let's see them sort that one out! Muahahahaha!"

Mom: **"MUAHAHAHAHA!"**

Me: **"MUAHAHAHAHA!"**

Dad: "Muahahahaha!"

Dad never did perfect his evil laugh, which I feel is at least partially to blame for his lack of success.

My mother, Irene the Unmerciful-Incomprehensible, was herself the product of an extremely evil home. The youngest of three sisters, she grew up in Talbot, New Mexico, where her parents, Zolvax and Marie the Unmerciful, had settled down after numerous failed attempts at superheating the Earth's core in an effort to melt the polar ice caps.

Like many mothers when I was growing up, Mom didn't work outside the home. She helped Dad out, evil-wise, whenever possible (her homemade mind-control pies were a big reason he was voted into office in the first place), and she was quite fond of using Dad's advanced technology around the house.

"Aw, man . . .
genetically altered broccoli again?"

I also had a younger brother whom I'll refer to as "Kyle", since that was his name. Kyle was a delightful child. As he approached his fifth birthday, he had already proven himself to be a polite, courteous, and helpful young citizen. He was put up for adoption shortly thereafter.

I received less-than-stellar grades from elementary school through junior high, not because I wasn't staggeringly intelligent (I was), but because I spent every waking moment plotting the downfall of the entire school district.

L. LEMENTARY ELEMENTARY SCHOOL
GOMERSBOROUGH, WISCONSIN
GRADE 4

The start of my high-school career coincided with Dad finally unveiling his XZ7000 Remote Laser Cannon, which he was fond of publicly boasting was so accurate it could burn a hole the diameter of a crocheting needle clean through a human skull—say, that of a high-school teacher—from its orbit nearly twenty-three thousand miles above the Earth's surface. I received excellent grades in high school.

I went on to study a couple of semesters at Duke University, where I continued to hone my evil as a member of the Blue Devils basketball team. I never actually got to play in a game (apparently I wasn't "tall" enough, even *with* my Helmet of Disconcertment), but I do still hold the single-game record for most injuries inflicted upon an opponent through "incidental" contact involving a scorer's table (six).

I left college when the opportunity arose to join the Denizens of Doom, at the time the top evil Supervillain organization in the world. They had an opening for a Lackey in their Minion Division. I remained with the DOD for seven years, rising as high as Assistant Human Resources Manager. And then "the incident" occurred. Due to ~~a huge blunder an enormous lapse in judgment~~ circumstances that were completely beyond my control, I failed to conduct a thorough enough background investigation prior to hiring a new Supervillain named Commander Vice. It turns out he was actually Commander Virtue with a different colored mask and some hair gel. Again, honesty does not appear to be one of his virtues. After that presumptuous pinhead single-handedly destroyed half of the DOD secret lair, it was mutually agreed that I would pursue other employment opportunities. Needless to say, they eventually regretted letting me go.

"On the off chance that I'm not the only person who bought this book, how can more than one of us become the ruler of the world at the same time? And if some other ambitious evildoer does beat me to it, am I entitled to a refund?"

Why, you sound like a whiny little ingrate!

THIRD COMMANDMENT OF INCOMPREHENSIBILITY

Crush any whiny little ingrates you happen to stumble across. I mean literally *crush* them. I have found that a 1993 Honda Accord dropped from a retro-fitted army surplus helicopter will accomplish the task quite satisfactorily.

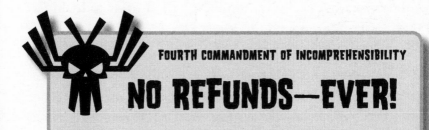

FOURTH COMMANDMENT OF INCOMPREHENSIBILITY

NO REFUNDS—EVER!

Alas, I grow weary of responding to your blabbering, even when it offers me the opportunity to rave about myself. The previous question represents a clear decline in intelligence, even for you, which is disappointing but hardly surprising. I have, therefore, decided to end my introduction here.

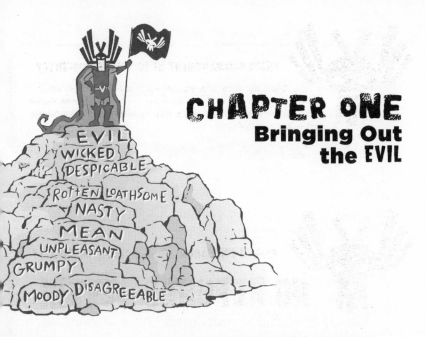

CHAPTER ONE
Bringing Out the EVIL

I grew up in a corrupt, vengeful, spite-filled environment of extreme wickedness and unspeakable evil. Not everyone was as fortunate. Since a blackened soul is a must for becoming the **EVIL RULER OF THE WORLD**, hopeful planetary tyrants will need to bring their own deep-seeded diabolism to the forefront.

In this chapter I will make an attempt, which will no doubt prove successful, to develop or "grow" the evil that exists like a boil inside of you and everyone else. That's right—*everyone*. It may not be much at the moment, but with the proper pricking and scratching, that little boil of evil will be transformed into an *infected sore* of evil, a *rotting, oozing, stinking, dripping* . . . Well, you get the idea. Actually, knowing you, you probably don't.

As a matter of fact; I can sense you whining and sniveling already:

"Oh, yeah? What about Santa? Santa isn't evil.
Santa doesn't have an evil bone in his entire jolly old body."

Oh, really? Tell me, what would you call someone who:

a) Commands easily frightened little toy-makers who have no other career options if they wish to remain in their North Pole homeland?

b) Leaves ponies and jet skis and solid gold Xbox 360s under the tree for children from extremely wealthy families who already have all that stuff anyway, while *your* meager haul of presents consists mainly of underwear?

c) Has only *one* suit . . . which he wears *every* day . . . which means Mrs. Santa has to wash it every night?

I'll tell you what I call him—*an evil genius*! And he has you completely bamboozled (big surprise, there). Any other examples of purity and goodness you would like to throw out there?

Well, how about Mr. Quimby? He owns the ice cream shop in town. He's a super nice guy and he gives away all his ice cream for FREE!

Ah, yes. Mr. Quimby. Did you know his first name is Vlad?

Care to try again? (Hint: Correct answer = no)

"No, I guess not . . ."

No, I guess not who?

"No, I guess not, your evil incomprehensibleness."

That is truly pathetic! Try again, this time in a lettering style worthy of my immense immensity and overall ginormousness.

"No, I guess not,

Your Evil Incomprehensibleness."

Well, then, it looks like we finally agree that everyone has at least a small measure of evil within them. Perhaps next time you won't waste my valuable time arguing. I realize you have nothing better to do, but consider that your insolence has wasted nearly an entire page—space I had originally intended to use to teach you how to transform Cheerios into gold using an ordinary vacuum cleaner. Ah, well—your loss.

FIFTH COMMANDMENT OF INCOMPREHENSIBILITY

Arguing with Vordak the Incomprehensible will result in a decided shortage of gold on your part.

On the bright side, you *will* have more Cheerios.

The challenge now becomes to increase that evil to the monumental level necessary to become the **RULER OF THE WORLD! MUAHAHAHAHA!** Perhaps you have noticed that no one currently rules the world, even though there are plenty of bad guys out there who would give their mother's right arm to do so. Do you know what these bad guys lack that keeps them from **RULING THE WORLD?** Extreme Villainy In Large Quantities, or **EVILQ**, which, if we take away the **Q**, leaves us with **EVIL**, which is what we're talking about here. The truth is, even the worst of the so-called "evil masterminds" just aren't evil *enough* to take over the world. This is great news for you, as it leaves the door to planetary domination wide open.

So, how does one become more evil? By making others' lives miserable. That's really all evil is—saying or doing something that brings misery to others. And every evil act you commit will serve to aggravate that boil of evil a little bit more until it ultimately consumes you, at which point the world will be within your grasp.

Think of yourself as a container that you will need to fill with evil in order to eventually **RULE THE WORLD!** Right now you probably have only a little bit of evil in you—say, up to your ankles. Every villainous act you commit will add a bit more evil to the container, raising the level ever so slightly until it eventually reaches the top of your head. At this point, assuming no leakage through your ears, your brain will be completely immersed in evil, thus corrupting your every thought, word, and deed. This will take a long time and will require a great deal of evil-doing, but the result will be a diabolical scoundrel capable of conquering the planet. And, yes, I just *knew* this next question was coming:

"What if I hang upside down? Then all the evil will flow into my head and cover my brain much sooner."

You no doubt consider this a brilliant observation on your part. Unfortunately, there are two problems with your plan:

1. Hanging upside down long enough will cause your head to explode.

2. Which will make it extremely difficult to read the remainder of my book.

As with anything worth achieving, the road to all-encompassing evil has no shortcuts.

COMMITTING ACTS OF EVIL

As I pointed out earlier, for an act to be considered truly evil it must inflict misery or misfortune on others—both if things go just right. Therefore, a particular phrase may or may not be evil, depending on the circumstances. For example:

Not Evil

"Wow! You are one fat cow.
I'll bet the butcher can't wait to get ahold of you!"

Evil

"Wow! You are one fat cow.
I'll bet the butcher can't wait to get ahold of you!"

The same hold true for actions:

This action, by itself, is **not** evil.

CLICK!

However, when this same action results in a button being pushed . . .

Screeetch!

. . . which activates an enormous gate-lifting mechanism . . .

GRRRRRRR!

. . . which releases a monstrous creature from the bowels of the Earth . . .

SLURP!

. . . which proceeds to destroy a major metropolitan area . . . that *is* evil.

You have probably noticed that this page is printed upside down. You also probably assumed this was a mistake on my part (your insolence has been duly noted).

Well, you assumed wrong!

I did it intentionally so that anyone who sees you holding your book upside down will naturally assume you possess the brains of a turnip. Now you feel like a complete ignoramus, which means that I, Vordak the Incomprehensible, have executed yet another staggeringly effective act of evil. And I must admit, doing so still makes me feel all tingly inside!

Obviously, I do not expect you to devise such works of brilliance right off the bat (if ever), but you need to start spreading misery immediately if I am to have any hope of your becoming evil enough to rule the world during my lifetime. For this reason, I have included a sampling of my highly sought-after "three ways to" series of evil plots, plans, and schemes, many of which I, myself, put to use as a youngster. These will allow you to begin building your inner evil right away while you continue to devise your own dastardly deeds for later use.

VORDAK THE INCOMPREHENSIBLE'S
Three Ways to Make a Girl Scout Cry

1. Tell her that her uniform makes her butt look big.

2. When she isn't looking, staple a "Boy, am I ugly!" award patch to her vest or sash.

3. When no one is looking, use a Sharpie to alter the cookie boxes in her sales display.

VORDAK THE INCOMPREHENSIBLE'S
Three Ways to Ruin a Field Trip to the Zoo

1. Sneak on to the bus early and superglue all the windows shut. Then make sure that Arnie "the Armpit" Kradmeister, who showers only on national holidays, sits directly in front of the heater.

2. Beg your teacher to perform her very best baby seal impression. Then use your handheld matter transmitter to immediately teleport her into the polar bear exhibit.

3. Relocate the sign for the petting zoo to a more "interesting" location.

VORDAK THE INCOMPREHENSIBLE'S
Three Ways to Make Your Little Brother
Look Like an Idiot

1. Volunteer to help him get dressed in the morning.

2. Weld the handlebars on his tricycle so they no longer turn and aim him directly at a telephone pole.

3. Teach him that the word for shoes is "poop".

"I gots poop on my feet! I gots lots more poop in my closet, too!"

VORDAK THE INCOMPREHENSIBLE'S
Three Ways to Torment the Elderly

1. Sneak into your local nursing home when everyone is asleep and mix up all the false teeth.

2. Tell them how easy they had things when they were kids.

3. Place signs offering free meals in strategic locations throughout the community.

VORDAK THE INCOMPREHENSIBLE'S
Special Bonus Sure-fire Way
to Make Your Mother Pass Out

Disclaimer: If you are stupid enough to actually stick the fork into the electric outlet, your run toward world domination will be a short one.

Additional Disclaimer: I am not responsible for any injury your buttocks may sustain due to forceful and repeated contact with your mother's shoe when she finds out you are uninjured.

While you are building your evil on the inside, it is also important to evilize your outward appearance. You want the hapless troglodytes who populate this planet to know you reek of evil even if you don't happen to be doing anything diabolical at the moment.

THE EVIL LAUGH!

You have no doubt noticed that I embellish statements of particularly high diabolicalness with a spine-tingling laugh of pure unadulterated evil. It tends to be somewhat overused within today's Evil Masterminding community, but, when delivered correctly, the evil laugh still has the ability to make anyone, from the most insignificant slug to the most powerful world leader, soil their trousers in fear.

Regardless of the age of the cackler, a well-practiced evil laugh can transform even a perfectly ordinary phrase into a sinister statement of unimaginable evil. Take the following harmless comment:

"I'm going to take my bike out for a spin."

No big deal, right? Well, look with dread at what happens when we include a well-rehearsed evil laugh:

"I'm going to take my bike out for a spin. **MUAHAHA-HAHA!!!**"

It now becomes obvious to anyone within earshot that your little excursion will include kicking over garbage cans, running small children down from behind, and tossing flaming torches on to neighborhood rooftops.

Along with your costume (Chapter 2—and don't even *think* of looking ahead), your evil laugh will go a long way toward determining just how seriously the rest of the world takes you as a would-be planetary conqueror. Therefore, you must begin developing it immediately. In a moment I will demand that you laugh loudly, clearly, and *evilly* directly into the highly advanced, two-dimensional, page-mounted transmitter I have provided below (yet another publishing first). It is linked directly into my helmet's likewise highly advanced communications system, allowing me to analyze your laugh and provide you with constructive feedback. Okay, commence evil laughter . . . *now*!

... I'm sorry.* Commence means begin. I should have made that clear.† So, let's try this again—commence (begin) evil laughter ... now!

... I'm still not hearing anything ... and I'm fairly certain I know what the problem is.

SIXTH COMMANDMENT OF INCOMPREHENSIBILITY

When attempting to communicate using a highly advanced, two-dimensional, page-mounted transmitter, it helps a great deal to push the ON button first.

Well, go back to the transmitter and turn it on—and don't fiddle with the other switches! Then, lean in real close and try again. And speak up, for zounds' sake! Don't worry if bystanders give you odd looks—you will have plenty of time to deal with them once you **RULE THE WORLD! MUAHAHAHA!**

... Well, that is truly odd. I still can't hear you. I wonder what the problem could possibly be *now* ...

SEVENTH COMMANDMENT OF INCOMPREHENSIBILITY

There is no such thing as a highly advanced, two-dimensional, page-mounted transmitter.*

* YOU IMBECILE

---

* THAT YOU ARE SUCH AN IMBECILE
† SINCE YOU ARE SUCH AN IMBECILE

YES! That is twice now that I have made you look like a complete dolt in this chapter alone. Zounds, I love being evil! Zounds, I am so darned good at it! Zounds, I love saying "zounds"! I'm tempted to clone myself right now just so I can pat myself on the back. Could you possibly have doubts any longer that I am the right choice to teach you the ways of Evil Mastermindery?

Now, where were we? Ah, yes—evil laughter. An evil laugh is a very personal attribute. Like snowflakes, no two are exactly alike. Also like a snowflake, it is capable of sending a shiver down the spine. Unlike a snowflake, you can't form a bunch of evil laughs into a ball and hit someone in the back of the head with it. You should practice your laugh in front of a mirror until you find a stance and sound that you are comfortable with.

Here are a few tips:

Evil Laughter Tips

- Hands should be on hips or rolled into fists and thrust in the air, never in your pockets.

- Tilting your head back will open up your throat, giving your evil laugh a crisper, cleaner sound.

- No snorting. Your laugh will lose its effectiveness and you are likely to attract hogs.

EVIL MANNERS

I assume you were taught to be polite as a show of respect for others. Well, as an Evil Mastermind you don't have any respect for others because there are no others worthy of your respect. You are superior to those around you, and you had better start acting like it. For example:

• Never ask—*demand!*

No

"Pardon me, Miss Shtorberhausen, but may I please be excused to use the restroom?"

Yes

"Attention, Miss Shtorberhausen and insignificant members of the seventh-grade social-studies class at Robert High Jr. Junior High. I will be taking a brief leave of absence to tend to personal matters that are of no concern to you. You will refrain from engaging in any instructive activities until such point as I return to the classroom. That is all."

• Never say "thank you"—rather, *berate the individual for a job poorly done!*

Classmate:

"EXCUSE ME, YOU DROPPED THIS BOOK WHEN YOU WERE CLOSING YOUR LOCKER."

You:

No

"OH, THANK YOU!"

Yes

"WHAT?! YOU SAW THE BOOK FALL FROM MY HAND, YET DID NOT SACRIFICE YOURSELF BY DIVING TO CATCH IT BEFORE IT TOUCHED THE FLOOR?! SEE HOW SMALL DUST PARTICULATES NOW CLING TO ITS COVER? YOU WILL CLEAN IT THOROUGHLY AND RETURN IT TO ME PRIOR TO FIFTH PERIOD OR SUFFER DIRE CONSEQUENCES INDEED!"

THE MANY FACES OF EVIL

You should also work to perfect the many evil facial expressions you will be called upon to exhibit during a typical day of wickedness and persecution. Here are a few that I have developed to the point of perfection over the years:

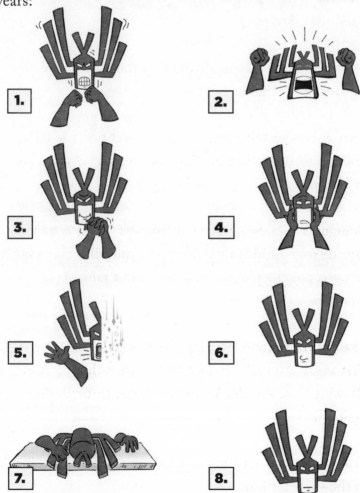

1. **Enraged Astonishment** that some impudent worm has dared to question you.

2. **Diabolical Glee** at seeing an evil plan come together.

3. **Devious Anticipation** for the unveiling of your latest doomsday device.

4. **Disappointment** on realizing that there is no one on this planet to challenge you.

5. **Fury** that your teleportation device went on the fritz midway through transporting you to your vacation lair in Hawaii.

6. **Smugness** in knowing that Commander Virtue is standing directly over a hidden trapdoor that you will momentarily activate, thereby plummeting him into a tank of angry piranhas.

7. **Exasperation** upon learning that the piranhas weren't all that angry after all—in fact, they were rather pleasant, allowing Commander Virtue to escape through the tank's filter.

8. **Frustration** that wearing an iron helmet makes it difficult to show frustration.

So, Are You Evil Enough to Rule the World Yet?

Well, there is only one way to find out. When you have completed this chapter, go back to the introduction and retake my Evil Aptitude Exam. If you achieve a high enough score, you may proceed to Chapter 2. If not, I will meet you back at the beginning of this chapter and we will go through everything again. On second thought, you can go through it again by yourself. If I become any more evil, I'll burst.

THE EVIL PLEDGE

I would like to end this chapter by sharing with you a special pledge. So I will. It was handed down through my family for generations. No one knows who started it, but since I am the first to take the time to write it down and put a nice border around it, it shall from this point forward be known as Vordak the Incomprehensible's Prodigious Pledge of Evil. Recite this every morning when you awake to assure that you will do your best to do your worst in the day ahead.

Vordak the Incomprehensible's Prodigious Pledge of Evil

AS I WAKE THIS MORNING
TO BEGIN ANOTHER DAY,
I PLEDGE TO BE NEFARIOUS
IN WHAT I DO AND SAY.

I'LL BE OBNOXIOUS, MEAN, AND SPITEFUL,
LOATHSOME, HEINOUS, VERY BAD,
A MALIGNANT EVIL PRESENCE,
A MALICIOUS, AWFUL CAD.

I WILL HECKLE, TRICK, OR TORMENT
EVERY PERSON WHOM I MEET,
AND SOMETIMES I WILL DO ALL THREE
A FIENDISH, NASTY FEAT.

AND WHEN I HIT THE SACK TONIGHT
EXHAUSTED, STIFF, AND SORE
I'LL SURELY BE MORE EVIL
THAN I WAS THE NIGHT BEFORE.

CHAPTER TWO
Getting a Jump on Your EVIL Career

What is the first thing that popped into your mind when you saw this bombastic book radiating its brilliance from the shelf of your local bookstore?

"I never should have had that 87-ounce Dr Pepper for lunch. I wonder where the bathroom is in this place."

INCORRECT! You were thinking that the book's author must be unimaginably powerful and immeasurably evil based on the picture and name displayed on the front cover.

"No, I definitely had to go real bad."

Of course you did. My visage on the cover intimidated you to the extent you nearly wet your pants.

"No, I just really had to—"

ENOUGH, ALREADY! You were scared, and that's that. I get the last word because I wrote the book. Which reminds me you were also thinking how ruggedly handsome I must be beneath my helmet. But mainly you were scared and intimidated by my name and appearance. Why? Because that was my intention. In this chapter, I will help you craft your own evil persona with which to unleash your reign of terror upon the planet. I will also show you how to make the money necessary to get your evil operation off the ground.

SELECTING A GUT-WRENCHINGLY EVIL NAME

The key to gaining immediate respect is selecting a name befitting a feared being of immeasurable power and evil. Face it—no one is going to grovel at the feet of Myron Snortsberger, even if he does possess the ability to reduce an entire hemisphere to smoldering ash. And the satisfaction derived from groveling masses is a huge part of what we're trying to accomplish here in the first place. Creating an intimidating Evil Supervillain name takes a sharp mind and a strong vocabulary . . . so I will do it for you. Simply follow the directions provided in my inconceivably evil Evil Name Generator

VORDAK THE INCOMPREHENSIBLE'S
Inconceivably Evil Evil Name Generator

Any Evil Supervillain name worth an aardvark's patoot is made up of four parts, which I shall designate as part one, part two, part three, and part four. Try and keep up.

Part One:

Part one is, obviously, your first name. Not your current first name—that one is totally lame. Your parents chose it because it means "courageous friend" or "honorable son" or some such ridiculous thing. Or you may have been named after your grandparent or great-grandparent, in which case you have an old person's name. Either way you are going to require something much more evil. To assure you don't screw this up, I have provided you with the template below. Each and every letter shown has undergone stringent testing to assure its evilness. Take your time and be sure you are pleased with your selection. Remember—this is the name that will go on the inside of all your underwear waistbands.

DIRECTIONS:
1. SELECT ONE LETTER FROM EACH COLUMN.
2. DO NOT REPEAT ANY LETTERS.
3. DO NOT EVEN *THINK* OF USING **VORDAK**.

V			M		G
K			K		Z
T			Z		K
Z	O	L	N	A	R
M	A	R	D	O	X

YOUR NEW EVIL FIRST NAME: ☐ ☐ ☐ ☐ ☐ ☐

Part Two:

The second part of your new name is *the* (pronounced "thee"). It is always *the*. Under no circumstances imaginable should it ever be anything other than *the*—never, never, ever! It absolutely, positively must be *the*.

"What about Kenneth?"

ACK! Perhaps you recognize my expression from the previous chapter! I am really beginning to hate my thought-anticipation powers.

Part Three:

Otherwise known as the third part, part three of your evil name is invisible and silent. It is not to be written or spoken under any circumstances ever. No one must know what it is, including you.

Part Four:

Now it is time to bring your new name home with a flourish, to let all the incompetent troglodytes who populate this planet know just what it is about you that makes you so vastly superior to them. Clearly, *Incomprehensible* is the single most awe-inspiring fourth part of an Evil Supervillain name ever conceived of. It is absolute perfection. Merriam-Webster defines it as follows:

> *In-com-pre-hen-si-ble*: having or subject to no limits, impossible to comprehend.

That's right—impossible! So don't even try. Here are a few evil name fourth parts which I deem acceptably intimidating for you to use. If you wish to add a bit more extravagance, use two of them together, adding an "ly" to the end of the first (example: *Unyieldingly Fearsome* or *Fearsomely Unyielding*).

Ruthless	Impatient	Unjust
Fearsome	Vengeful	Impure
Unmerciful	Obnoxious	Uncompassionate
Heartless	Diabolical	Unyielding
Unaffectionate	Monumental	Unforgiving
Omniscient	Unrelenting	Magnificent

Notice you don't see *Incomprehensible* anywhere in this list. It goes without saying that you may not use *Incomprehensible* as part of your own Supervillain name. But I went ahead and said it anyway. That's just how incomprehensible I am.

Putting It All Together

When you have decided on a name that you feel is sufficiently frightening, say, Zolnax the Unrelenting or Malzor the Unyieldingly Heartless, enter it on the form on the next page (and also on the Standard Evil Promise of Employment Agreement on page 14). Of course, you are also free to ignore my advice completely and select a name yourself—just don't come crying to me when people aren't lining up to bow at the feet of Doug the Mildly Unfriendly.

(part 1)	THE (part 2)	(part 3)	(LY) (part 4) (optional)	(part 4) (required)

Even though, technically, your name is still "Kyle Witmeyer" or "George Jones" or "Shannon Peterman" (at least until you can legally change it on your eighteenth birthday), you should begin flaunting your new evil name as soon as possible. Practice speaking and reading it until it rolls off your tongue and leaps off the page. Then use it when introducing yourself and answering the phone (and don't be afraid to throw in a bloodcurdling evil laugh every now and then). Write it on all of your stuff. Sign it on all of your school papers. And, perhaps most important, begin slipping it casually into everyday conversation:

Wrong:

"I'm thirsty. You want to go grab a Slurpee, Stanley?"

Right:

"I thirst! Accompany me, Mordax the Unmerciful, to 7-Eleven, you insignificant gastropod!"

THE SUPERVILLAIN COSTUME

I am a staunch believer in the "pretentious costume" approach to evil apparel. The more flamboyant the better. Others, including Lex Luthor and Dr. Evil, have managed to wreak planet-threatening havoc while wearing far less conspicuous attire. Is one style necessarily superior to the other? Of course—mine is, which is why I will be focusing primarily on pretentious costume design. Now, let's take a closer look at the major elements of your dastardly designer duds:

LAWN & GARDEN

A well-designed Supervillain costume serves to intimidate the hapless masses while also allowing the elusive evildoer to blend seamlessly into his surroundings when necessary.

Color Scheme

If you intend on becoming a seriously nasty Evil Supervillain, you have four basic options for your principal costume color:

DARK BLACK

BLACK

LIGHT BLACK

DARK DARK
DARK DARK
DARK GRAY

Bad guys wear black. That's just how it is. Sure, you could try wearing a bright, colorful costume. You could also try eating a bucket of nails. Both would display the same level of intelligence on your part.

You: *"BEHOLD, WORTHLESS SCUM! I AM KARNOX THE UNYIELDING AND I DEMAND THAT YOU KNEEL BEFORE MY AWESOME MIGHT!"*

Worthless Scum: *"DUDE, THOSE ARE SOME SERIOUSLY SWEET BLUE-AND-YELLOW THREADS YOU'VE GOT THERE. LET ME GUESS . . . YOU'RE A SUPERHERO, RIGHT?"*

You: *"A SUPERHERO?! WOULD A SUPERHERO DEMAND THAT YOU KNEEL BEFORE HIS AWESOME MIGHT?"*

Worthless Scum: *"IF HE'S STUCK UP, HE MIGHT. I DON'T KNOW—I'VE NEVER MET A REAL LIVE SUPERHERO LIKE YOU BEFORE."*

You: *"I'M NOT A SUPERHERO! A SUPERHERO CERTAINLY WOULDN'T REFER TO YOU AS WORTHLESS SCUM NOW, WOULD HE?!"*

Worthless Scum: *"IF HE WAS PERCEPTIVE, HE MIGHT. I MEAN, I AM PRETTY LAZY WHEN YOU GET RIGHT DOWN TO IT."*

You: *"ENOUGH! I AM KARNOX THE UNYIELDING AND I INTEND TO CONQUER THIS PLANET AND RULE IT IN A HIGHLY EVIL MANNER!"*

Worthless Scum: *"HEY! YOU LOOKING FOR A SIDEKICK? ALL THE SUPERHEROES HAVE 'EM, AND I'M NOT EXACTLY BUSY AT THE MOMENT."*

You: *"AAAARRGGHHHH!!"*

This doesn't mean you can't add a splash of color here and there to provide a bit of zip to your ensemble, but the predominant hue should be black. Black is the color of hopelessness, of despair, of oppression. Black is the corner of a basement in the dead of night, the space under the bed where the light doesn't reach, the shadowy recesses of an unlit closet. Black represents the pall of darkness that your evil rule will cast over the planet. It is also quite slimming, particularly if you incorporate vertical stripes into your design.

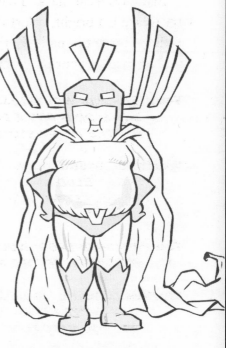

A white costume can make even the most fit of Supervillains appear a bit, umm, lumpy.

Mask

When it comes to cranial coverings, there are a number of options available. The following chart highlights the pros and cons of the most popular facial fashions:

EVIL SUPERMENACE MASK SELECTION CHART	SINISTER APPEARANCE ACHIEVED VIA FACIAL HAIR	BREATHING DIFFICULT	PRESERVES SECRET IDENTITY	PROTECTS FACE FROM SUPERHERO PUNCHES / KICKS	HIDES FACIAL DISFIGUREMENTS	HINDERS EATING	MAKES VERBAL COMMUNICATION DIFFICULT	LEAVES BRAIN SUSCEPTIBLE TO
NO MASK	YES	NO	NO	NO	NO	NO	NO	NO
PARTIAL MASK	YES BUT MASK MAY HELP	NO	ONLY WHEN DEALING WITH MORONS	NO	ONLY IF EYE RELATED	NO	NO	NO
FULL MASK	NO	NO UNLESS AIRTIGHT MATERIAL USED	YES	NO	YES	YES	NO	N(
METALLIC MASK & COWL	NO	YES	YES	YES	YES THAT IS OFTEN ITS MAIN PURPOSE	YES	YES	NO
HELMET	NO	NO	YES	TO EYES & FOREHEAD YES — TO MOUTH & CHIN NO	POSSIBLY	NO UNLESS BOBBING FOR APPLES	NO	NO
PLEXIGLAS-ENCASED BRAIN ATOP ROBOTIC BODY	NO BUT MAY BE APPLIED WITH A SHARPIE ANYWAY	YES DUE MAINLY TO LACK OF NOSE & MOUTH	YES ASSUMING YOU HAVEN'T PREVIOUSLY SHOWN ANYBODY YOUR BRAIN	WHAT FACE?	SEE PREVIOUS COLUMN	NO THANKS TO LIQUID-NUTRIENT-DELIVERY SYSTEM	DEPENDS ON QUALITY OF VOICE-SYNTHESIS UNIT	YES UNLE: PROPE: PROTEC

Clearly, the only headgear worthy of adorning the haughty head of an ambitious world-swallower is the illustrious helmet. The name of the game is intimidation, and your helmet must strike fear into all who gaze upon it. Practicality is not a consideration. Take my incredible Helmet of Disconcertment, for example. It's heavy, hot in the summer, cold in the winter, difficult to see out of, and loud as heck when something hard clangs off it. But you must admit, the mere sight of its magnificent splendor causes your knees to buckle and your stomach to turn inside out* (seriously, admit it or put the book down right now). Plus, it has built-in speakers for my iPod.

A well-designed, easily recognizable helmet will also allow you to cast terrifying shadows and create frightening doorway silhouettes, both of which will come in handy when you wish to make a dramatic entrance.

---

* I TYPICALLY AVOID LOOKING IN THE MIRROR FOR FEAR I WILL ACCIDENTALLY INTIMIDATE MYSELF.

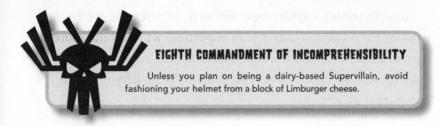

EIGHTH COMMANDMENT OF INCOMPREHENSIBILITY

Unless you plan on being a dairy-based Supervillain, avoid
fashioning your helmet from a block of Limburger cheese.

Cape

Cape or no cape? That is the question. Cape. That is the
answer. And here is why:

> **CAUTION:** *Advanced logic is about to be applied. To avoid looking like a
> complete cabbage-head, say "Ah, yes" and nod understandingly after reading
> point number 4.*

1. Darth Vader wears a cape.
2. The Riddler does not.
3. Darth Vader is much more evil than the Riddler.
4. Therefore, a cape makes a Supervillain more evil.

Actually, a high-quality cape will make anyone more of whatever it is they already are. A Superhero will become more heroic, a magician will become more magical, a professional wrestler will become more . . . professional wrestlery—all simply by wearing a cape.

Obviously, I am in favor of anything that will make you more evil. If standing on your head and farting the theme to *SpongeBob SquarePants* made you more evil,* I would tell you to do that, too. So a cape is a must. They come in all shapes and sizes, but I prefer mine to be long and flowing for dramatic effect. Nothing says "I am important" quite like sitting astride your horse atop a mountain peak while your cape blows majestically in the breeze— not that that particular opportunity comes along very often.

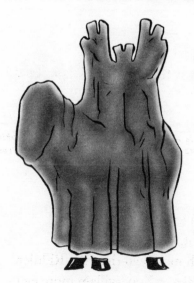

Strong, steady breezes are great for majestic cape blowing. Sudden wind gusts, not so much.

* AND I DON'T SEE HOW IT COULDN'T

When worn properly, a cape will add a certain amount of flair and pizzazz to a Supervillain costume. And therein lies the key—it must be worn properly. Be prepared to spend many hours practicing to perfect the various flamboyant gestures and sweeping motions necessary to achieve the maximum benefit from your cape.

NINTH COMMANDMENT OF INCOMPREHENSIBILITY

When wearing a long, flowing cape, never let a bumbling oaf walk directly behind you.

Boots

As the saying goes, "You can tell a man by the shoes he wears." Well, the same holds true for an insidiously evil man who hopes to someday RULE THE WORLD!!! Note how the elegant design of my own fantastic footwear alerts all to my magnificence. Regardless of the material or style of your boots, they should include a solid heel to generate intimidating sounds as you walk through the vast echoing hallways of your secret lair and a steel toe for added oomph when "booting" the hindquarters of a hapless henchman.

Tip: Scented inserts will help absorb unfortunate yet unavoidable foot odor—it can get awful warm in those boots, especially if the soles house miniature propulsion jets.

Gloves

Gloves are an essential part of any Supervillain costume as they are on full display whenever you conduct dramatic hand gestures, which is pretty much all the time. Whether made of metal or highly advanced synthetic materials, your gloves must provide freedom of movement to push buttons, pull levers, turn dials, make fists, fire handheld weapons, and form the "No. 1" sign when you are caught on camera at a sporting event. They must also be of suitable construction to protect your hands from mishap. My own gloves are extremely flexible yet rugged enough to prevent biting injuries when I attempt to pet my dog, Armageddon. Stylistically, your gloves should complement your boots to some degree. Functionally, they need to be water, acid, lava, and booger repellent. They should also be sticky enough to improve your grip when dangling from a ledge or catwalk, but not too sticky to make everyday activities troublesome.

Too sticky

Tip: You may choose to equip your gloves with energy beams, shrink rays, freeze rays, or other weaponry, but be forewarned—you will need to be extremely careful when going to the bathroom.

Utility Belt

Many Supervillains overlook the importance of the utility belt when designing their costumes. For example, this guy:

That's right—a utility belt not only holds things, it holds things *up*. I learned the value of a well-stocked utility belt years ago. Thirty-seven separate times I had Commander Virtue caught in the clutches of one of my diabolically clever yet extremely slow-acting death traps, only to see him yank some ridiculous little item out of his belt and free himself at the last moment. Needless to say, it didn't take me thirty-eight to figure out that I, too, needed a utility belt. Now I have one of my own that I wear at all times, including in the shower (it's where I keep my soap).

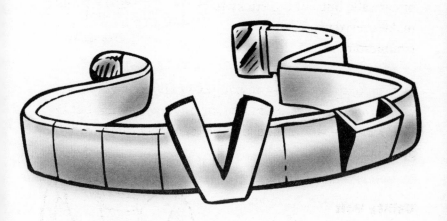

Below you will find my Staggeringly Complete Utility Belt Contents Checklist, which you may use to supply your own belt with all the random items a true Master of Evil might find useful in a pinch. Obviously, the chubbier you are, the more storage compartments you will be able to fit on your belt.

VORDAK THE INCOMPREHENSIBLE'S
Staggeringly Complete Utility Belt Contents Checklist

- ❏ Utility knife
- ❏ Invisibility tablets
- ❏ Flashlight
- ❏ Cell phone
- ❏ Sulfuric acid
- ❏ Breath mints
- ❏ Plasters
- ❏ Chapstick
- ❏ Toothbrush
- ❏ A Sharpie
- ❏ Needle and thread
- ❏ Compact death ray
- ❏ Spare batteries for compact death ray
- ❏ Moist towelettes
- ❏ Wallet
- ❏ Two live scorpions
- ❏ Aspirin
- ❏ 2x3 photograph of arch-nemesis
- ❏ Pretzels
- ❏ A spare utility belt
- ❏ A small mirror
- ❏ Deodorant
- ❏ Smoke pellets
- ❏ A magenta crayon
- ❏ Keys to lair
- ❏ iPod
- ❏ Kleenex
- ❏ Assortment of mini grenades
- ❏ Sunscreen
- ❏ Loose change for vending machines
- ❏ Poisonous gas capsules
- ❏ Starburst fruit chews

Spare Costumes

Remember to keep plenty of spare costumes on hand. You never know when battling a Superhero, feeding one of your dreadful creatures, conducting laser experiments, or engaging in some other dangerous activity might tear, soil, or otherwise damage your dastardly duds and make a quick change necessary.

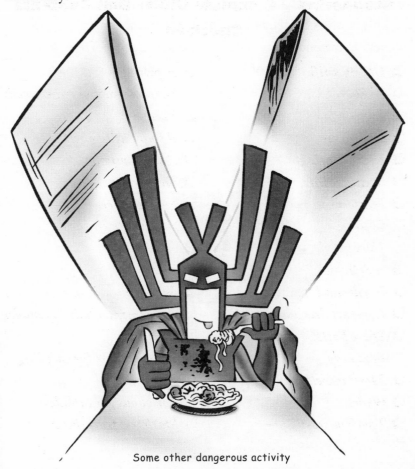

Some other dangerous activity

Costume Variety

I find it helpful to have a number of specialized costumes to wear when circumstances dictate. As breathtakingly magnificent as my everyday ensemble is, I must admit it feels good to don different adornment on occasion. After all, variety is the spice of life.

This is my formal costume, to be worn only when accepting planetary surrender . . . or while posing for this portrait. Gaze upon it in short bursts or its brilliance will drive you mad.

Here I am in my aquatic costume. I wore this frequently while headquartered in my sub-oceanic lair. Michael Phelps, eat your heart out.

And, of course, something for the more casual moments between evil escapades. (By the way, my flaming liver dogs were always a huge hit. No one ever complained twice.)

RAISING MONEY

All right, so there you are, an evil young person with a terrifying new name and an awe-inspiring new costume, standing ready to strike fear in the hearts of the wretched ranks of humanity. So what's stopping you? Money. Or, rather, a lack of it. Nothing of real, lasting, world-impacting evil can be accomplished without a great deal of money. Lairs must be built. Supervillains need to be paid. Nightmarish weapons, elaborate vehicles, and diabolically clever yet extremely slow-acting Superhero death traps must be designed and built. As if this chapter required any further wisdom to become immeasurably valuable, I will now offer you a few tips for raising cartloads of cash.

As you become more powerful, you will think nothing of issuing multibillion-dollar ultimatums to nations across the globe. Since you are just starting out, however, you need to set your sights a bit lower. Here are a few evil techniques to help wring big profits from small businesses:

Lemonade Stand
1. Choose a location with a proven customer base.
2. Reduce the cost of your ingredients.
3. Discourage competition.
4. Increase your profit per unit.
5. Make your product irresistible to customers.
6. Sit back and count your money.

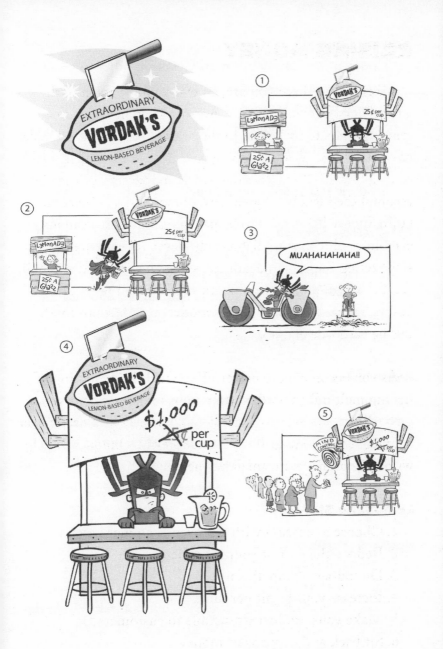

Mowing Lawns

- Undercut the competition price-wise in order to generate a staggering number of customers.
- Collect the full season's fees in advance.
- Sabotage underground sprinkler systems, cut holes in hoses, and use highly advanced weather-control devices to prevent rain, thus guaranteeing grass won't grow.
- Sit back and count your money.

Pet-Sitting Service

- For a reasonable fee, agree to watch customers' pets while they (the customers) are away from home.
- Send customers a ransom note demanding $500 each for the safe return of their furry little creatures.
- Sit back and count your money.

Babysitting

- Similar procedure to pet-sitting.
- For a reasonable fee, agree to watch customers' children while they (the customers) are away from home.
- Send customers a ransom note demanding ~~$500~~ $350 each for the safe return of their ~~furry~~ snotty little creatures.
- Sit back and count your money.

Bottle Returns

Nothing diabolical here, but you might want to give it a try, anyway. If you live in a state with bottle and can deposits, you receive 5¢ for every one you return. Do the math—20 million cans = *1 million dollars!*
MUAHAHAHAHA!!!

This concludes chapter 2. To determine whether you were paying attention, I have prepared a little exercise for you. Using your now-keen eye for costume design, select the pulse-pounding portrait below in which my attire is slightly different from the others. If you succeed, you may proceed to chapter 3. If not, you must reread the costume section—and this time take notes!

(answer on the following page)

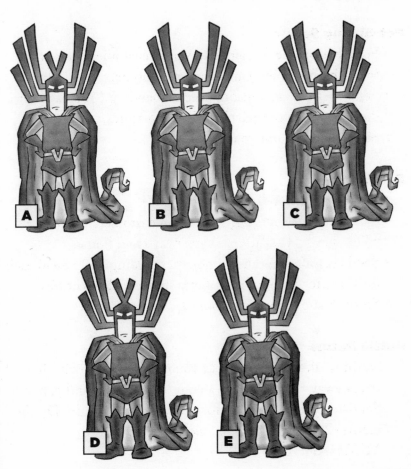

Answer: D

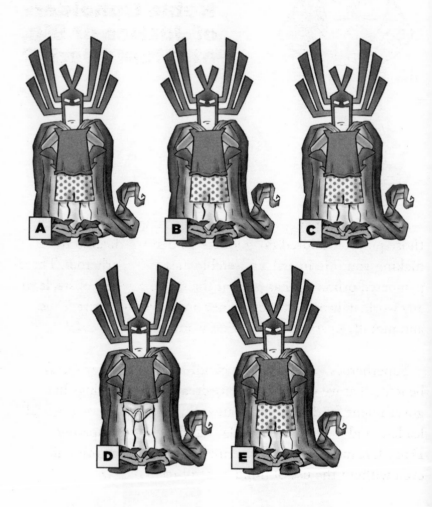

CHAPTER THREE
SUPERHEROES—
Noble Upholders of Justice or Big, Fat, Stupid Jerks?

The priceless pages of this cherished chapter will focus on those publicly adored do-gooders who are dedicated to making your life in evil a miserable mess—Superheroes. These pampered prima donnas present the single greatest obstacle to any world-takeover attempt. They are powerful, courageous, and morally upstanding. In other words, *incredible jerks*!

Superheroes get everything handed to them. They receive benefits that we villains can only dream about—things like government funding, the private cell phone numbers of world leaders, and half-price hot fudge sundaes at participating Dairy Cream locations. They are also idolized by millions, even without the use of mind-control technology.

Superheroes have it easy in the overall good vs. evil scheme of things. We Evil Masterminds work long, grueling hours developing our organizations and concocting our brilliantly evil plans, patiently biding our time for the ideal moment in which to strike. And then, in swoops the Superhero to thwart everything. No preparation. No planning. Nothing. He simply receives "the call" and off he goes, swooping and thwarting. And if I have to listen to one more of these haughty heroes drone on about how evil never wins and how I'll be spending the rest of my life behind bars, I just may regurgitate my lunch.

> **"Umm, not to question your judgment,**
> Your Evil Incomprehensibleness,
> **but shouldn't we learn about lairs and weapons and vehicles and stuff before we deal with Superheroes? It's not like they're going to come after us until we begin to threaten the world anyway, right?"**

So, you say you are not going to question my judgment *and then go right ahead and question it, anyway!... (must ... control ... rage)* ... Using a spoon, fashion my likeness from a four-foot-tall wheel of Muenster cheese, display it in your bedroom for six weeks, **AND PRAY THAT THAT WILL PROVE SUFFICIENT TO APPEASE MY ANGER!** It would have been Limburger, but I gave you a break for using the proper dramatic font for my title.

The reason we are discussing Superheroes now rather than later is precisely because they will not wait until you become world-threateningly powerful to begin pestering you. Once word gets out that you have decided to dedicate your life to evil, those gladiators of goodness will be all over you like flies on poop*, especially once you begin wearing your costume.

---

* YES, IN THIS EXAMPLE YOU ARE THE POOP—AND DESERVEDLY SO.

A Quick Word About Diabolically Clever Yet Extremely Slow-Acting Death Traps

Before I continue, I need to briefly mention diabolically clever yet extremely slow-acting death traps. Although these devilish devices will be covered in more detail later in the book, I believe it is important that you get a basic trap up and running as soon as possible. The Superhero community will soon be aware of your existence, so you never know when you'll have a subdued foe in need of leisurely destruction.

Here is a simple yet effective Superhero death trap that should hold you over until you have the time and money to develop more ingenious devices. You can set it up in your own yard using ordinary items you can find lying around:

Name of trap: Rodent's Revenge
Type of trap: Slowly lowering to ultimate doom
Effective for: Superheroes weighing less than 250 pounds
What you will require:

Assemble as follows:

What Is a Superhero?

That is an excellent question, which is not surprising, since I am the one who asked it. To answer, let's take a closer look at what the word *Superhero* actually stands for:

Stupid

Ugly

Pig-kissing

Earwax-eating

Rear-end-scratching

Handkerchief-licking

Elephant-snot-flinging

Rump-sniffing

Old buttface

"So what's the big deal, then? They don't sound so tough to me. I mean, I sit next to a handkerchief-licking earwax eater in my second-period science class, and he gets beat up every day on the way home from school . . . by a girl . . . who's in kindergarten."

Well, unfortunately, most Superheroes also possess some type of superpower such as tremendous strength, or a highly advanced skill like superhuman marksmanship with a bow and arrow. You would need an *army* of kindergarten girls to defeat just one of them, and imagine how much that would cost in juice boxes alone.

Besides the unfortunate physical gifts, Superheroes also possess a ridiculously strong moral fiber, far beyond that of the ordinary citizen. Since I am fairly certain you have no idea what I am talking about, let's take a look at an example—say, how various types of people would react to a house that is on fire.

- **Ordinary citizen:** Call 911.

- **Upstanding citizen:** Call 911 and run down to the end of the street to help direct fire trucks to the endangered domicile.

- **Superhero:** Intercept the 911 call, speed to the location of the fire, stop briefly en route to foil an attempted bank robbery, arrive at the scene, place fists against hips and exclaim, "Have no fear, MR. SPECTACULAR is here!", rush inside and rescue everyone plus any pets and family heirlooms, use Super Breath* to extinguish the blaze, pose briefly for photographs, lecture bystanders on the dangers of leaving small appliances turned on, retrieve the neighbor's cat from a tree, tell everyone to have a nice day, and return to secret headquarters for a quick shower before bedtime.

* OR THUNDER CLAP

Now that you have made the decision to dedicate your life to taking over the world, this is the type of individual you will be forced to deal with. Every. Single. Day. The good news is you can get a head start on defeating a number of them by memorizing the information I am about to give you. These are overviews of Superheroes with whom I am nauseatingly familiar. They include inside information that will prove invaluable should you run into any of these appalling upholders of justice somewhere down the road. These summaries come from my very own superspecial top secret index-card file. (I have been planning to transfer the information to my Vordax 12000DX Supercomputer, but I need to remove a couple of games first.) I have personally battled each of these moralizing miscreants, so you can rest assured that the information is accurate.

THE AMAZING TODDLER-MAN

IDENTITY: Todd Lerman

ORIGIN: Was bitten on the hand by a radioactive two-year-old

POWERS/STRENGTHS: Possesses the proportionate strength, agility, and snot production of a two-year-old. Strength (and snot production) multiplies hundredfold when having a temper tantrum. If he closes his eyes, you can't see him.

WEAKNESSES: Will eat anything. Gets cranky after 7:30 p.m. Requires afternoon naps. Has been known to "drop a stinky" while battling adversaries. Poor balance.

WEAPONS/ACCESSORIES: Will pick up and throw objects he finds lying about, usually after putting them in his mouth first.

NOTES: Easily lured into diabolically clever yet extremely slow-acting death traps with cookies, candy, or music from *Dora the Explorer*.

THE THONG

IDENTITY: Ben Grimace

ORIGIN: Believed to have been bombarded with cosmic rays while piloting the space shuttle through an asteroid field with the windows down.

POWERS/STRENGTHS: Cosmic rays transformed him into a rocklike creature with incredible strength and near invulnerability.

WEAKNESSES: Same cosmic rays also shrank his pants, which frequently "ride up," causing him to release adversaries from his powerful grasp in order to pull the shorts out of his "rocky crevice".

WEAPONS/ACCESSORIES: None

NOTES: He's very self-conscious about his appearance. Calling him names like Brick Breath and Boulder Butt can really throw him off his game.

THE ARTFUL CODGER

IDENTITY: Old Man Crenshaw

ORIGIN: While Crenshaw was in his early seventies, the Supervillain Young Whippersnapper cut in front of him in a grocery store line. He vowed revenge on all evildoers.

POWERS/STRENGTHS: Eighty-three years old, but thanks to a modest exercise program, possesses the strength, speed, and digestive system of a man ten years younger.

WEAKNESSES: Easily confused. Often forgets who he is battling and why. Drives his Codger Mobile at extremely slow speeds and leaves his indicator on.

WEAPONS/ACCESSORIES: Has been known to use his cane to poke adversaries in their midsections.

NOTES: If you happen upon his secret headquarters, don't even think of walking on the grass.

THE OTTER

IDENTITY: Unknown—no one has ever bothered to find out.

ORIGIN: Average guy decided he looked good in an otter costume.

POWERS/STRENGTHS: None come to mind.

WEAKNESSES: You name it.

WEAPONS/ACCESSORIES: Does not appear to use/have any. You would think he might stick to the whole "otter" theme and, for example, use rocks to crack open Supervillain skulls—but no.

NOTES: Aside from Inchworm, this is probably the least intimidating of all Superheroes. Enjoys delivering clever catchphrases such as "You *otter* know better than to tangle with the Otter". Drives an Otter Mobile.

NARWHAL

IDENTITY: Not sure, but I'm thinking it might be this guy.

ORIGIN: Unknown

POWERS/STRENGTHS: A master swordsman who uses his horn-like tooth to disarm and subdue adversaries. Can change TV channels from his chair without using the remote.

WEAKNESSES: Tooth makes it difficult to open doors, ride in cars, or sit in crowded movie theaters. It is also cavity prone since he can't reach the end of it with his toothbrush.

WEAPONS/ACCESSORIES: Blowhole may be equipped to discharge tear or knockout gas.

NOTES: Tooth-based speech impediment makes his witty banter difficult to understand.

ARROWHEAD

IDENTITY: Unknown

ORIGIN: Unknown

POWERS/STRENGTHS: Slightly above average strength, speed, and agility due to a lifetime gym membership.

WEAKNESSES: The fact that he is completely blind really hinders his accuracy.

WEAPONS/ACCESSORIES: Bow and a vast array of specialty arrows.

NOTES: Can easily avoid his arrows by disguising yourself as the door of a barn.

AQUA STAN

IDENTITY: Prince Stanley, Lord of the Deep

ORIGIN: Unknown

POWERS/STRENGTHS: Incredible strength when in water. Can telepathically communicate with all forms of sea life, although all he knows how to say is, "Yo, what's up?" Pretty good swimmer.

WEAKNESSES: Has strength of a wet sock on dry land. Tastes good to sharks.

WEAPONS/ACCESSORIES: Trident is equipped with paralysis beam. It is also extremely pointy. Has trained numerous sea creatures to serve as underwater transportation, although none larger than a crab.

NOTES: Easily lured into diabolically clever yet extremely slow-acting death traps with minnows, shiny lures, or small pieces of hot dog.

LEAD MAN

IDENTITY: Toby Clark, billionaire industrialist

ORIGIN: A brilliant inventor, Clark was kidnapped by terrorists and built the lead suit in order to escape. No one is quite sure why he didn't use the ultrathin, ultrastrong, ultralight titanium, which was sitting on the shelf right next to the lead.

POWERS/STRENGTHS: The suit is virtually indestructible and provides Clark with superhuman strength.

WEAKNESSES: Can barely move, even with superhuman strength, due to the tremendous weight of the suit. Sweats a lot. Chafing a real problem.

WEAPONS/ACCESSORIES: Chest-mounted power beam, visor-mounted disintegration ray, wrist-mounted rocket launchers.

NOTES: Don't worry about the wrist-mounted rocket launchers—he can't lift his arms to aim them at anything.

LIEUTENANT COLONEL AMERICA

IDENTITY: Roger Stevens

ORIGIN: As a volunteer, he was injected with a secret experimental serum by top American scientists in an effort to create a supersoldier. This originally angered Stevens, as he was under the impression he was volunteering to give blood.

POWERS/STRENGTHS: Brilliant military strategist and master of hand-to-hand combat. Can lift up to three times his own body weight, depending on what he had for breakfast. A dynamite acrobat—can do six somersaults in a row.

WEAKNESSES: Stops whatever he is doing and places his hand over his heart whenever he hears "The Star-Spangled Banner". Due to a design flaw, his shield has a large hole in it.

WEAPONS/ACCESSORIES: The Shield of Truth, the Billy Club of Justice, and the Utility Belt of the American Way.

NOTES: Boasts of being the most patriotic American on the planet, but his costumes are made in China.

THE ARCH-NEMESIS

And then there is (sigh) Commander Virtue. You will find that as your stature as an Evil Mastermind grows, so, too, will the attention directed toward you by the Superhero community. And chances are there will be one particular hero who has decided to dedicate his life to defending the world from *you*, specifically. This individual is known as your arch-nemesis and he can be a real pain, believe me. Commander Virtue is *my* arch-nemesis and, as such, has been a throbbing ache in my evil backside for decades.

I still remember the first time our paths crossed like it was yesterday. I had recently completed a long-range temporary shrink-ray prototype and was about to give the world a demonstration of my might by reducing the entire population of Merrimack, New Hampshire, to half size. I had put a *lot* of work into this particular evil scheme. The shrink-ray cannon was lubricated and fully charged, the satellite properly aligned, and the United Nations patched in via closed-circuit television to witness the event. Just as I pressed the Fire button and let loose with my most intimidating evil laugh (**MUAHAHAHAHA!**), who should appear swooping down out of the sky but Commander Virtue, sun gleaming radiantly off his freshly polished costume.

The beam deflected off his chest directly back toward me and, without going into great detail, let's just say I had to buy my underwear at GapKids for the next few months.

That marked the beginning of a long and tiresome relationship. I would set the wheels of some nefarious scheme in motion—Commander Virtue would swoop in at the last minute to thwart it. Swoop and thwart. Swoop and thwart. Man, I hate that guy.

Why Him and Why You?

So just what is it that will cause a particular Superhero, an individual you may not even know, to become so obsessed with stopping you at every turn? There are any number of possible reasons, most of which aren't even your fault, including:

- You unwittingly kidnapped his mother/grandmother/ sister/girlfriend/dog while collecting hostages to ransom for billions of dollars in gold bullion. (Not your fault.)

- You unknowingly leveled his secret headquarters while clearing land for the construction of your fabulous new lair. (Not your fault.)

- You accidentally disintegrated his entire hometown while demonstrating the awesome power of your latest doomsday device. (Not your fault.)

- You mocked his appearance before the entire world, saying you haven't seen an outfit that tight since

Lance Armstrong let Jack Black borrow his biking shorts. (Okay, this one is probably your fault.)

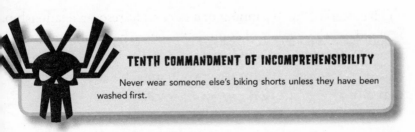

TENTH COMMANDMENT OF INCOMPREHENSIBILITY

Never wear someone else's biking shorts unless they have been washed first.

As far as which one of these actions may have spurred Commander Virtue to latch on to *me* with such vigor I can't really say, seeing as I did them all.

Communicating with your Arch-Nemesis

If there is one thing a Superhero enjoys more than anything about battling a Supervillain, it's the clever dialogue. Well, he probably enjoys punching the Supervillain repeatedly in the face a bit more, but that's it . . . aside from trashing the Supervillain's lair. And maybe beating up his henchmen. But clever dialogue is definitely right up there.

Since you will be facing off against your own arch-nemesis with great frequency, it is important that you learn to hold your own in the verbal arena and not become trapped in his web of clichés. Take the following example of a cliché-filled exchange between a Supervillain and his arch-nemesis:

STOP RIGHT THERE, SCOUNDREL!

I'VE BEEN EXPECTING YOU.

 YOUR DAYS OF VILLAINY ARE OVER!

I'M AFRAID YOU'RE TOO LATE!

IT'S *NEVER* TOO LATE . . . FOR *JUSTICE!*

SOON THE WORLD WILL BE MINE!

 NOT ON MY WATCH! TAKE *THAT!*

OUCH!

 AND *THAT!*

OOOMF!

 AND *THAT!*

AAACK!

 HAD ENOUGH, EVIL ONE?

HA! IS THAT THE BEST YOU CAN DO?

 TRY *THIS* ON FOR SIZE!

UUGHH! OKAY! ENOUGH! I GIVE UP!

 CRIME DOES NOT PAY!

I GUESS NOT. JUST LET ME GRAB MY CAPE.
IT'S OVER THERE BY THE ESCAPE POD.

NOT SO FAST!

DRAT! FOILED AGAIN!

SO, YOU THOUGHT YOU COULD OUTSMART ME!

YES, AND I WOULD HAVE, TOO, IF IT
WEREN'T FOR THOSE MEDDLING KIDS!

Notice how things turn out poorly for the Supervillain. Things always turn out poorly for the Supervillain when he foolishly tries to engage his Superheroic adversary in standard, cliché-filled rhetoric. Superheroes excel at this kind of thing. It's the only way they know how to talk. It's up to you, as the Supervillain in the room, to mix things up in order to knock that haughty hero off his stride. For example:

 STOP RIGHT THERE, SCOUNDREL!
I'VE BEEN EXPECTING YOU.

 YOUR DAYS OF VILLAINY ARE OVER!
YUP. YOU GOT ME. GREAT WORK.
WOULD YOU CARE FOR A MANGO SMOOTHIE?

 IT'S NEVER TOO LATE FOR JUS . . . HUH?
A MANGO SMOOTHIE. THEY'RE DELICIOUS!
WOULD YOU LIKE ONE?

 NOT ON MY WATCH! TAKE THAT!
OW! HEY! WHAT'D YOU DO THAT FOR?

 SORRY. HABIT, I GUESS.
WELL, YOU ALMOST KNOCKED THE SMOOTHIE
OUT OF MY HAND, FOR CRYING OUT LOUD!

 MANGO, YOU SAY?
YESSIREE.

 I LIKE MANGOS.
WELL, THEN, HERE YOU GO!

MMM! THIS IS DELICIOUS!

INDEED!

 SAY, I'M BEGINNING TO FEEL A BIT DROWSY . . .

INDEED!

 LET ME GUESS—YOU PUT SOMETHING IN THE SMOOTHIE, I'M GOING TO PASS OUT, AND YOU'RE GOING TO PUT ME IN ONE OF YOUR DIABOLICALLY CLEVER YET EXTREMELY SLOW-ACTING DEATH TRAPS, RIGHT?

INDEED!

 DRAT.

Note the difference. If, for some reason, you just don't feel truly evil unless you utter a few clichés yourself, wait until after your arch-nemesis has been secured in your diabolically clever yet extremely slow-acting death trap. You may then throw a few out there as you reveal the details of your nefarious scheme per regulation 7.1b of the Superhero/Supervillain Official Rules of Etiquette:*

---

*THIS SET OF REGULATIONS WAS AGREED UPON DURING A SECRET MEETING HELD MANY YEARS AGO. UNFORTUNATELY, THE HEROES WERE REPRESENTED IN THAT MEETING BY CAPTAIN ATTORNEY, RESULTING IN RULES SUCH AS REGULATION 7.1B, WHICH HAS BURNED ME MORE TIMES THAN I CARE TO REMEMBER.

drop him on top of his head repeatedly until such time as he remembers.

Regulation 7.1b—In the event a Supervillain subdues a Superhero, said Supervillain must reveal the complete details of his evil plan to said Superhero prior to "disposing of" him/her. This may be accomplished either through direct dialogue between the two parties or by allowing the Superhero to eavesdrop on the Supervillain as he summarizes his plans via an egotistical rant to no one in particular. Should said Superhero subsequently manage to escape, he or she is free to use this information as he or she sees fit.

Regulation 7.1c—In the event both a Superhero and his sidekick are captured simultaneously, they must be secured back to back in a manner which allows the sidekick access to the Superhero's utility belt. This will provide the Superhero a fair chance to

A Quick Word About Sidekicks

As difficult as this may be to believe, there is actually a living organism on this planet that irritates me more than the Superhero.

"Do you mean . . . me?"

All right—two living organisms. And the other one is the Superhero sidekick, a pint-sized pain in the rear who is just like a real Superhero except that he's younger, smaller, and doesn't have any superpowers. He still wears a costume, but it's not . . . now how shall I put this . . . as "rugged" as that worn by his grown-up counterpart (think Peter Pan booties). His fighting ability is about the equal of two henchmen, and his vocabulary consists mostly of exclamations like "Holy Moly!" "Gee Whiz!" and "Jumpin' Jehoshaphat!"

Not every Superhero has a sidekick, but those who do keep them around for three reasons:

1. To warn the Superhero that a Supervillain is sneaking up on him from behind.
2. To help the Superhero escape from the grasp of diabolically clever yet extremely slow-acting death traps.
3. To wash and wax the SuperMobile.

On the plus side, they make excellent hostages. There is no stronger bait with which to lure a Superhero into your clutches than a kidnapped sidekick.

"How come Supervillains don't usually have sidekicks?"

Because we would just kidnap them. It's what we do.

That concludes the chapter on Superheroes. Now that you have read it, I am sure you will agree that its pages contain nearly unimaginable amounts of wisdom. Close the book and put it in a safe place for a few days before beginning the chapter on lairs—it is equally remarkable and I am afraid that reading the chapters back to back will cause your head to explode. It may, anyway. If so, e-mail me and I will send you a robotic replacement head (indicate size: S, M, or L).

"Pardon me,
Your Evil Incomprehensibleness,
**but could you give us just one final tip for defeating Superheroes
before we proceed to the next chapter?"**

Very well. You have behaved yourself fairly well since that little mishap at the beginning of the chapter, so I present you with ...

Just One Final Tip for Defeating Superheroes Before We Proceed to the Next Chapter

Mock the Superhero's name during battle. If you are fighting The Mighty Trooper, for example, you might call him The Mighty Pooper. Skylark would be Skidmark, Commander Comet would be Commander Vomit, and so on. This lack of respect *really* ticks them off and often causes them to come unglued.

CHAPTER FOUR
The EVIL Lair

EVIL AVE

LAIR LANE

NEIGHBORHOOD WATCH

PROGRAM IN FORCE
Working together to help prevent captures

If you wish to be taken seriously as an Evil Supervillain, and the very fact that you are reading this titanic tome tells me you do, you *must* have a lair. This heinous hideout will serve as your headquarters for worldwide evil operations. Within its confines you will hatch your sinister schemes, utter ulcer-inducing ultimatums, create wickedly warped weapons, punish ham-handed henchmen, and take noteworthy naps—not to mention hold hapless heroes captive in your diabolically clever yet extremely slow-acting death traps.

TOP SECRET OR LOUD AND PROUD

Perhaps the trickiest decision facing any hopeful EVIL RULER OF THE WORLD is whether to keep the location of his lair a secret or to include an awe-inspiring likeness of himself somewhere in its design. I have always leaned toward the "awe-inspiring likeness" side of things but, then again, with a likeness such as mine, who wouldn't? Here are a few photographs that demonstrate what I am talking about. I inhabited these incomparable strongholds during my "national landmark" lair phase. Feel free to gaze upon them in disbelief—I certainly do.

Palace of Westminster—Big Ben
This stylish lair had a great location in the heart of London. Unfortunately, no one informed me that it had a huge bell in it, and the repeated clanging forced me to relocate.

Eiffel Tower
This enormous edifice of evil was
probably my most graceful lair.
Also my least well thought through—
I realized shortly after moving in
that the tower actually has no interior.

Mount Rushmore
Had I succeeded in taking over the
world while headquartered here, I
had planned to transform the other
three heads to my likeness, as well.

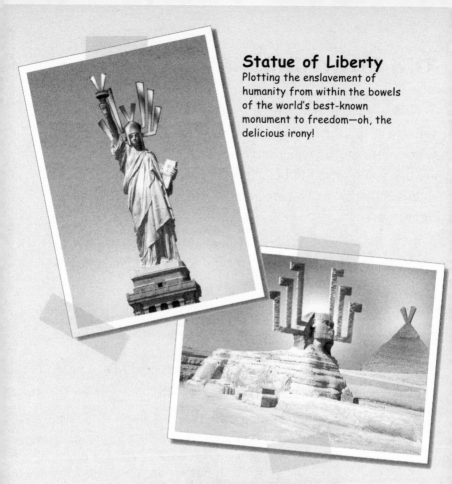

Statue of Liberty
Plotting the enslavement of humanity from within the bowels of the world's best-known monument to freedom—oh, the delicious irony!

Great Sphinx
I don't know what I was thinking here—I mean, it's smack dab in the middle of the desert, for crying out loud.

So, as you can see, secrecy has never been a big deal for me. Some have said that is why my repeated attempts to conquer the world have ~~fizzled flopped bombed failed miserably~~ come up just a wee bit short, but I still insist it was due to circumstances that were completely beyond my control.

THE STARTER LAIR

Now, are you going to be able to run right out and build yourself a lair as glorious as those you have just witnessed? Of course not. You are just a sniveling, whiny little goober, after all. But you do need to begin plotting your evil schemes as soon as possible, so you are going to need some sort of lair right away.

I would suggest you start out with something basic, like your bedroom:

With some minor alterations, you can have a bedroom lair up and running in no time. Then, once your career in evil begins to pick up steam, you will be able to upgrade gradually to more fiendishly magnificent command posts, as I did:

VORDAK THE INCOMPREHENSIBLE'S
Evil Lair Gradual Upgrade Chart

TYPE OF LAIR	HOW I PAID FOR IT
BEDROOM	SAVED UP BIRTHDAY MONEY
TREE HOUSE	CUT WIDOW BRITTLEBUN'S LAWN
CONVERTED GARAGE	BAGGED GROCERIES AT SMART MART
GEOSYNCHRONOUS DOOMSDAY-CLASS ORBITING SPACE STATION	RECEIVED $100 BILLION RANSOM FROM THE LEAGUE OF NATIONS AFTER THREATENING TO USE MY INCONCEIVABLE EVAPORATION RAY TO COMPLETELY DRAIN THE ATLANTIC OCEAN

"Okay, but how will I know when it's time to move into a bigger lair? Do you have a list of four signs or something that you could share?"

A list of four signs is exactly what I have! You obviously looked ahead and for that you will pay most dearly. Write *I am unworthy of Vordak's incomprehensible wisdom* fifty thousand times, one sentence per page and mail it to me **IMMEDIATELY!** Only then may you stare in breathless wonder at:

VORDAK THE INCOMPREHENSIBLE'S
Four Signs That You May Have Outgrown Your Current Lair

1. There is a long line outside the only henchman-punishment chamber.
2. You have to add a card table to the end of your Conference Table of Iniquity in order to seat everyone.
3. Your Supervillains are sleeping in bunk beds.
4. Your current lair looks like this:

There, now wasn't that worth the hand cramps?

CHOOSING THE LAIR THAT'S RIGHT FOR YOU

Once you have carried out a few evil schemes, spread a fair amount of misfortune, and made a bit of a name for yourself, it will be time to move into a truly sinister lair worthy of your ever-expanding evil. But what type will you choose? Should your lair be belowground or above? And if above, how far above? Should it be mobile or firmly rooted in place? Should you enter your lair through a door or through a giant clown's mouth? You have a number of options, which I have taken a great deal of my valuable time to outline for you below:

The Abominable Abandoned Waterfront Factory

Located in the heart of henchman breeding grounds, abandoned waterfront factories provide plenty of space for vehicles, weapons, and banks of supercomputers. They usually come pre-furnished with a maze of catwalks to use during daring escapes, dangerous machinery that may easily be converted into Superhero death traps, and barrels of toxic waste that may be used to create horrific sludge monsters or to dip unsatisfactory henchmen into. They do tend to be a bit drafty in the winter, so you may wish to keep a sweater handy.

The Ominously Orbiting Space Station

If you happen to be a death-ray kind of guy (and what Super-villain isn't, really?), the space-based lair is perfectly situated to rain destructive beams of all shapes and sizes across the Earth's surface—while also offering spectacular views of the devastation. But that kind of fun does not come cheap: a fully equipped orbiting space lair can cost tens of billions of dollars, and that doesn't include toilet paper. **Tip:** If you decide to go this route, e-mail me and I'll show you how to rig your tsunami-beam energy collector to pick up TV signals.

The Medieval Mountaintop Stronghold

One of the true classics in evil lairdom. Its timeless stone construction makes it a popular choice to hand down from evil generation to evil generation. Dungeons abound, so you'll have plenty of space to imprison hostages and Superheroes awaiting placement in diabolically clever yet extremely slow-acting death traps. This impenetrable stronghold also comes with a moat that you can fill with your choice of crocodiles, piranhas, or body-dissolving liquids. **Note:** Climbing the steps to the entrance can be exhausting at times, especially if you are carrying groceries.

The Mysterious Moon Base

If you are looking for a quiet spot to relax and plot the downfall of humanity, you might consider constructing a futuristic moon base. You'll have plenty of room to expand, and the continuous view of the Earth will help keep you focused on the task at hand. And if your plans include the total destruction of a significant portion of the planet, you will be safely tucked away in a cozy crater some 240,000 miles away.

The only drawback, and it's a minor one, is that the moon has no atmosphere, so if your oxygen generator breaks down, you will die a horrible, painful, agonizing, ghastly death.

The Insidious Submarine

If you are intent upon seizing control of the world's oceans and don't mind eating fish sticks three times a day, the submarine lair may be just the ticket. Loaded to the gills with torpedoes, missiles, and other state-of-the-art weaponry, this submerged sanctuary will allow you to terrorize seagoing vessels the world over. **Tip:** Due to the recycling of air aboard the ship, I highly recommend that you institute a strict no-farting policy among the crew.

The Villainous Volcanic Island

Perhaps you are interested in a remote refuge where you will be free to perform your genetic experiments away from the bright lights of civilization. Well, here is just what the diabolical doctor ordered. Uncharted and brimming with ~~test subjects~~ island natives, the volcanic island lair is the perfect home base for your evil experimental endeavors. It also makes a great vacation lair. **Note:** These lairs are a lot more difficult to come by than you might think—it isn't easy finding an island with both a dormant volcano and a skull-shaped cave entrance that isn't also inhabited by a hundred-foot-tall gorilla.

The Uncanny Underwater Dome

If your plans for world domination include unleashing titanic tidal waves across the globe, I suggest looking into this deep-sea domicile due to its easy access to fault lines running along the ocean floor.

On the negative side, if the dome suffers even the tiniest crack, it will collapse upon itself and the resulting pressure will crush your head like a deflated soccer ball.

The Sinister Skyscraper Penthouse

Its prime location in the heart of the crowded city makes this soaring sanctum an excellent lair choice for those of you wishing to experiment with mind control or mass hypnosis. If you decide to go this route, make sure your lair has a large balcony so you can bombard the bustling bodies below with water balloons and loogies. **If Secrecy Is a Must:** Most Superheroes also live in the city, so I strongly urge you to keep an unlisted phone number.

The Glorious Gothic Cathedral

I, myself, once used an abandoned Gothic cathedral as my lair for close to three years. With its towering spires, intricately carved stonework, and spectacular stained-glass windows, it was truly a magnificent spectacle—much like myself. And its enormous rooms and soaring ceilings offered me plenty of space to store my many weapons, vehicles, and *Evil Supervillain of the Year* statuettes.

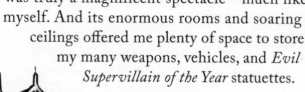

Bonus Feature: Most Gothic cathedrals also include a system of underground catacombs—perfect for making last-second escapes.

The Dastardly Deserted Amusement Park

If ridding the world of Superheroes is near the top of your list of goals, and why wouldn't it be, consider taking up residence in an abandoned amusement park and carrying out:

VORDAK THE INCOMPREHENSIBLE'S
Spectaculous Superhero Elimination Plan
(Deserted Amusement Park Lair Version)

1. Lure the Defender of Decency into your lair using a kidnapped sidekick or loved one as bait.

2. Use the park's assortment of mirror mazes and fun houses to confuse and disorient him.

3. Capture him and place him in a diabolically clever yet extremely slow-acting death trap that you created by altering one of the park's rides.

4. As he awaits his doom, calmly reveal the details of your plan to take over the world while munching on cotton candy.*

5. Repeat as necessary until all Superheroes have been disposed of.

* NO, YOUR PLAN IS NOT TO TAKE OVER THE WORLD WHILE MUNCHING ON COTTON CANDY.
YOU SHOULD *REVEAL* YOUR PLAN WHILE MUNCHING ON COTTON CANDY.

The Heinous Hovering Command Center

Like the submarine lair, this hovering hideout will keep the Superhero community scrambling to pinpoint your location. Unlike the submarine, you can drop bombs, poisonous liquids, and misbehaving henchmen out of it on to the unsuspecting masses of humanity below. On the downside, birds with sharp beaks are a known safety hazard, and this floating fortress gets only .000001 miles per gallon of hovering command center fuel.

The Unimaginable Underground Fortress

Sure, it doesn't look like much from the surface, but it's what lies below ground that matters. And what lies belowground is an extensive network of tunnels and caverns capable of housing your armies of evil minions. The underground lair is also ideal if you are intent on terrorizing the planet by superheating the Earth's core or unleashing gigantic creatures from the bowels of the Earth. Although a crypt entrance is shown here, tool sheds and dilapidated hunting cabins also make excellent secret entrances.

Caution: One known issue with this type of lair is that a single, well-placed explosive will send the entire complex collapsing in upon itself. And cell phone reception is nearly non existent.

A FEW FINAL WORDS OF ADVICE

The type of lair you choose and how you decide to furnish it is up to you. Yes, I could tell you exactly what to do every step of the way, and, yes, you would then end up with a far better lair—but it wouldn't really be your lair now, would it? It's all the stupid decisions you are going to make that will allow you to create a lair that is uniquely yours.

That being said, there are a few things I feel are important enough to mention. You are free to ignore this advice if you choose. Then again, I am free to seek you out and destroy your lair myself if you do.

- **Floors:** Should be made of tile, stone, wood, or metal to create intimidating echoes as you walk around. No carpeting! Be sure to wear boots with metallic heels and make sure everyone else wears rubber soles—you should be the only one echoing.

- **Ceilings and Doorways:** Should be extra high for Intimidating Helmet clearance.

- **Décor:** Statues and portraits are the only way to go, and your theme should be "ME, ME, ME". For example, take a look at one of my typical corridors from one of my typical lairs:

This is how you should decorate your own lair—and I don't mean with statues and portraits of yourself. I mean with statues and portraits of me, Vordak the Incomprehensible!

• **Bathrooms:**

All bathrooms should be self-cleaning and equipped with cape hooks and extra-large stalls to accommodate a wide variety of Supervillains, some of whom may not count hygiene among their powers.

- **Room Assignments:** If you intend on having the Supervillains under your command live full-time in your lair, use common sense when deciding who will share living quarters with whom. For example, and I tell you this from personal experience, don't let Earthquake and the Nitroglycerin Kid room together.

- **Conference Room:** You should have, by far, the largest chair at the table as a symbol of your superiority over the other Supervillains present.

• **Escape Pods:** The most important feature in any evil lair. If cornered by your arch-nemesis, you must have a way to flee and fight another day. Your escape pod should be large enough to hold only yourself and maybe a small pet—you don't want any uninvited passengers tagging along. Make sure you are just a step or two from safety at all times by placing escape pods every ten feet or so throughout your entire lair—and don't forget to outfit the escape pods with bathrooms (I learned this the hard way . . . don't ask).

"What do you mean you learned this the hard w—?"

I SAID, DON'T ASK!*

---

* YOU ARE *DARNED RIGHT* THAT LITTLE PIECE OF INSOLENCE IS GOING TO COST YOU! WRITE *I AM UNWORTHY OF VORDAK'S INCOMPREHENSIBLE WISDOM* FIFTY THOUSAND MORE TIMES, ONE *WORD* PER PAGE THIS TIME, AND MAIL THE PAGES TO ME IN SEPARATE ENVELOPES. NOT A VERY NICE WAY TO END A CHAPTER, NOW, IS IT?

CHAPTER FIVE
Building a Top-Notch EVIL Organization

An organization is only as good as the people in it. Fortunately for me, I myself have been a member of every organization I have ever been in, thus guaranteeing its success. You, on the other hand, aren't so lucky. In order to take over the world, you will need to surround yourself with good people, and by good people I mean, of course, bad people. Likewise, a bad person to surround yourself with would be a good person, since no good person is bad enough to be a good bad person, so you'll definitely want to avoid that.

This chaptabulous chapter's mind-numbing know-how will have you assembling a first-rate band of bad guys in no time.

ELEVENTH COMMANDMENT OF INCOMPREHENSIBILITY

From time to time it will become necessary to create a powerful new adjective, such as *chaptabulous*, in order to maintain your air of vocabulary superiority—particularly when you cannot find your Thesaurus of Evil.

We will begin by taking a look at STOP RIGHT THERE! DON'T ANYBODY MOVE!! I am sensing that a number of you ignoramuses have skipped ahead to this section of the book without even reading the previous chapters! If so, drop to the floor and give me one thousand sit-ups . . . while balancing a bowling ball on your head. Those chapters don't exist solely to allow me to bask in my own brilliance—I expect you to bask in it as well. On second thought, make it two thousand . . . and if you just rolled your eyes, add another five hundred. Now go back to the copyright page and begin reading again, memorizing every word—and let's just say you had better be wearing your acid-free Ethiopian ibex hair gloves.

For those of you who have read through the first 110 pages as intended, I will now tell you how to build your evil organization, a sinister staff of underlings who will provide you with:

- The numbers and firepower needed to carry out the abominable schemes you devise to take over the world.
- Someone to torment in the meantime.

MINIONS (10,000+ RECOMMENDED

These deplorable drudges occupy the bottom position on the totem pole and will be used to form your evil horde, your malignant multitude, your army of darkness. They can be frustrating at times, but at their best they are a relentless plague upon civilization. Minions lack ambition and are willing to do whatever is commanded of them, even though this might result in a severed limb or a lopped-off head.

A properly mastered minion horde is extremely useful for:

- Spreading fear among the general population.
- Battling the armies of stubborn, pesky nations.
- Creating a diversion so you can do something diabolical.
- Ganging up on Superheroes once control of the world has been established.
- Rounding out the rosters of your League of Evil softball teams.

You have a number of options available when it comes to choosing your minions, some costing more than others. Just beware—you get what you pay for.

BLIs (Beings of Limited Intelligence)

This group includes zombies, primates, and teenagers who wear their pants around their knees. They don't cost much to maintain and are easily kept under control by bombarding them with, in no particular order:

- Threats of physical torment.
- False promises that they will become important once you have gained control of the planet.
- Bananas.

The problem with BLIs is that their lack of intelligence makes it difficult for them to understand and follow directions, especially the teenagers. By themselves, BLIs are not very powerful, but send them out in groups of ten thousand or more and they will wreak some serious havoc. They tend not to bathe very often, so don't let them anywhere near your lair.

Clones

Clones are very expensive to produce because of the high cost of the cloning equipment. You will save some money on their uniforms, though, since they only have to be made in one size. Some Evil Masterminds choose to fill their minion armies with clones of themselves. Not me. Sure, the spectacle of ten thousand Vordak the Incomprehensibles would be a wondrous sight to behold, but I somehow think it would make me feel less special. Besides, one of me provides more than enough wonder as it is. Self-esteem *is* a major issue with clones, though, due to their lack of individuality. I, myself, solved this problem by starting a recognition program that greatly improved my clones' morale by making them feel "unique" and "special":

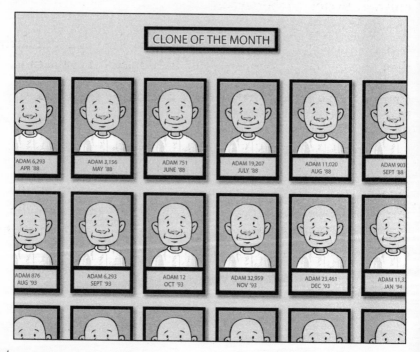

CLONE OF THE MONTH

ADAM 6,293 APR '88 — ADAM 3,156 MAY '88 — ADAM 751 JUNE '88 — ADAM 19,207 JULY '88 — ADAM 11,020 AUG '88 — ADAM 903 SEPT '88

ADAM 876 AUG '93 — ADAM 6,293 SEPT '93 — ADAM 12 OCT '93 — ADAM 32,959 NOV '93 — ADAM 23,461 DEC '93 — ADAM 11,3__ JAN '94

Programmable Entities

This category includes robots and cyborgs, which make ideal minions because they can be programmed with exact instructions to follow. Again, this is a very expensive way to go, especially if batteries are required. But an army of well-made mechanical monsters may be virtually invincible. In fact, it has been proven over the years that the only way to stop a robot/cyborg onslaught is for some Superhero to reprogram the units to turn against one another—and ultimately their creator—which happens roughly 100 percent of the time.

Demons, Devils, and Other Dark Creatures from the Underworld

I strongly recommend that you avoid this option altogether. Sure, it sounds tempting—unleashing these foul forces upon humanity—but you will have to spend months researching and memorizing spells designed to open an earthly portal from the underworld. And for what? So the first demon to come through can devour your soul and occupy your body's empty husk, free to enjoy the evil costume you worked so hard to design? I think not.

The Elderly

This group is often overlooked as a source of minionship. After all, unarmed old folks are certainly not as frightening as the other minions we've talked about—unless, of course, they're wearing their bathing suits. However, when equipped with their weapon of choice, the automobile, a few thousand of them can quickly send a major metropolitan area spiraling into complete chaos. The problem with this group is that they are extremely difficult to control. If you try to threaten them in any way, they will beat you senseless with their canes and hard black purses. My helmet has the dents to prove it. And mind control won't work on them, either, since what little working brain tissue they have left is used to store tales of how rough they had things when they were your age. Your only real option is to mail them phony senior citizen discount coupons to Denny's and watch them descend upon those restaurants like locusts on a cornfield.

I have always considered it important to rule my minions with an iron fist and inflict harsh discipline when I deem it appropriate, which is pretty much all the time. Any minions worth their salt will come to appreciate the foul treatment as proof that their existence, though nearly meaningless, is still worth tormenting—after all, you wouldn't punish needlessly if you didn't care. Case in point—I recently received this little surprise in my mind-boggling mailbox:

Dear Mr. Incomprehensible,

Hello! I hope this letter finds you in good health. You probably don't remember me, but I wanted to send you a note and let you know what an absolute privilege it was to have served as your minion. Since your retirement, I have bounced around from master to master and have had the good fortune to devour human flesh the world over. I must say, however, that that flesh seemed to taste just a little better when I was devouring it for you.

These days find me in rather high demand as a minion, a happenstance I attribute largely to the experience I gained while under your supreme evil mastery. And I want to assure you I hold no grudge whatsoever for the time you fed me to the sharks in a fit of rage. Quite the contrary, in fact, as it served only to make me work that much harder to overcome my newfound lack of a right arm and leg.

I have enclosed a recent photo of myself that may serve to refresh your memory, although when I last served you I believe my left nostril was still partially intact. Anyway, I will let you return to what certainly must be more important matters, but please feel free to summon me should you decide to resume your conquest of the planet.

All the best,

The Late Neville Farnsworth

Henchmen (Ten, Give or Take)

Also known as flunkies, stooges, lackeys, or thugs, henchmen are an important part of any successful evil outfit. They "fill in the gaps" between the widespread havoc wreaked by minion hordes and the highly specialized functions of Supervillains by providing such valuable services as:

- Robbing banks.
- Kidnapping.
- Guarding lair entrances.
- Picking up ransoms.
- Forming the initial, though easily dispatched, line of defense against Superheroes who gain entrance to your lair.
- Landscaping and snow removal.
- Dragging prisoners before you.
- Groveling.

High-quality henchmen usually come from among the ranks of petty criminals and other riff-raff of society. Unlike minions, most henchmen are normal-looking enough to mingle freely within the community, although their black turtlenecks and unshaven faces might look suspicious in most countries other than France.

Frenchmen   Henchmen

A properly trained henchman knows his place in the overall scheme of things. He understands that his life is not nearly as valuable as your own and that his role within your organization will require tremendous personal sacrifice. A worthwhile henchman must be willing, for example, to throw himself in front of an oncoming train in order to:

- Push you out of the way, thus saving your life.
- Distract bystanders, thus allowing you to secretly carry out some diabolical scheme or other.
- Slow it down, thus preventing its breeze from unnecessarily rustling your cape.

You will rarely require more than eight to ten henchmen at a time, but they don't last very long, so you will need to replace them often. Fortunately, there are people who can help you with this.

THE DISPOSABLE HENCHMAN
Temporary Agency

LOUIE THREE FINGERS
"ACQUISITIONS SPECIALIST"

789 KNEECAP DRIVE
Gotham Oaks, NY 08333
Ph(123)-555-3217

"WE SUPPLY THE HENCHMAN, YOU MAKE HIM TEMPORARY."

←—I used these guys. I found them to be extremely helpful and professional, especially after I implanted that remote-detonating explosive microchip in the base of Mr. Three Fingers's skull.

THE DISPOSABLE HENCHMAN
"Guarantee"

If you are unhappy with your henchman
for any reason, simply toss him into
a viper pit and we'll send a replacement.

PROUDLY SERVING THE EVIL MASTERMIND
COMMUNITY SINCE 1932

You should punish your henchmen often, even when they have done exactly as you commanded. This will keep them on their toes. And demand they address you as "Your Immenseness" or "Your Enormousness" to help remind them of their worthlessness compared to you.

A couple words of warning: henchmen have an annoying tendency to squeal like stuck pigs when they are captured and questioned by the forces of justice, so dole out information on a strictly need-to-know basis. They also can't aim handguns worth a darn. It seems the only things they can hit are open car doors, trash cans, and the ground. As you can imagine, this provides big laughs within the Superhero community:

Captain Purity:

"SORRY I'M A FEW MINUTES LATE, EVERYONE. I WAS CORNERED IN AN ALLEY BY A GANG OF VORDAK THE INCOMPREHENSIBLE'S ARMED HENCHMEN."

Garbage Can Man:

"BETTER YOU THAN ME!"
(hysterical laughter ensues)

Scientists (Twenty to Thirty)

Sure, they're dorky, but you will need them to monitor your magnificent banks of supercomputers and highly advanced weapons systems. You can easily lure these gangly geeks away from their regular jobs by promising them free pocket protectors and Star Wars DVDs. Equipped with white lab coats and clipboards, scientists look very impressive in the background when you issue video ultimatums to world leaders or give tours of your lair to captured Superheroes. However, should the forces of good ever manage to penetrate your lair's defenses, don't count on these eggheads to hang around and fight; they are easily spooked by sirens, flashing lights, and countdowns to self-destruction.

Supervillains (Ten to Twenty)

Much to my dismay, the world has become overrun with Superheroes. It's to the point where an Evil Genius can't even fire off a death ray these days without having it deflect harmlessly off the impenetrable pectorals of some deplorable do-gooder. Sure, you could tackle all these stalwart stiffs yourself, but that would take up valuable time better spent plotting the downfall of humanity.

Enter the Supervillain, a powerful being capable of battling the Superhero on even terms. More than even, one would think, since he is not bogged down by feelings of pity, compassion, and respect for human life—characteristics that often cripple the common Superhero. In a perfect world, this powerful Supervillain would defeat his Superhero adversary and return him to your lair for you to dispose of at your leisure using one of your diabolically clever yet extremely slow-acting death traps. Alas, the world is not perfect. If it was, I would be ruling it.

WHAT'S IN A NAME?

True story: I once hired a Supervillain who called himself "The Whizzer" because I naturally assumed he possessed superhuman speed. As it turned out, what he actually possessed was a bed-wetting problem. Here are a few other vapid villains I have come across whose actual abilities are not quite what I expected—consider yourself forewarned.

SUPERVILLAIN POWER CHART	ASSUMED	ACTUAL
Anaconda	immobilizes victims with inescapable death grip	eats without chewing
Señor Stretch	has deformable elastic body	"loosens up" extensively each morning
Professor Octopus	equipped with multiple powerful mechanical arms	squirts ink from bellybutton when frightened
Mr. Spectacular	possesses wide array of spectacular superpowers	thinks very highly of himself
Volcano	capable of violent emotional eruptions which leave massive destruction in their wake	remains inactive for decades at a time
StormCloud	controls the weather	negative personality brings others down
The Black Falcon	capable of winged flight	drives a black 1967 Ford Falcon
The Mad Magician	insane caster of powerful spells	an angry guy who does card tricks
Agent Ant	shrinks to ant size	enjoys ruining picnics
Atlas	possesses incredible strength	knows capitals of all 50 US states by heart
Madame Tarantula	mysterious and deadly international superspy	has hairy legs

Of course, there are also plenty of Supervillains running around whose powers are *exactly* what you would expect. This isn't necessarily a good thing, either, as you can see when you take the time to examine ...

VORDAK THE INCOMPREHENSIBLE'S
Legendary Listing of Supervillains to Avoid
(Unless, of Course, You Are a Superhero)

The Angry Gerbil
The Knock-Knock Joker
Cold Sore
Special Ed
General Malaise
Unclean Gene

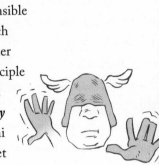

The Golden Puddle
The Scarlet Rash
Balsa Man
Glass Jaw
Hal Itosis
Aunty Social
Compost

Carl the Comprehensible
The Damp Match
Sergeant Surrender
The Dangling Participle
The Sticky Kid
The Blind Sentry
Screaming Mimi
The Wet Blanket
Sunburn
Lobotomy Boy
Captain Fragile
Nick Naked
Mr. Mucus
The Brown Smudge

At this point it should be obvious to anyone with an unsevered brain stem (and I'm going to go out on a limb and assume this includes you, but to be honest, I haven't been real impressed so far) that selecting Supervillains to add to your corrupt crew is not a task to be taken lightly. There are a lot of crappy villains out there, so you need to take the time to find those whose powers are both real and useful. Based upon the experience I have gained during my lengthy career in evil, I strongly suggest that any terrifying team you put together includes, at the very least:

A strong guy

I'm not talking "has the strength of ten men"–level muscle here. You need to secure the services of a Supervillain capable of leveling an office building with his bare hands, of throwing a bus across the Hudson River, of single-handedly wrestling a doughnut from the clutches of Homer Simpson. I struggled to fill this position early on in my career when the best I could manage was a villain named Rex Roider who, thanks to a six-month gym membership, could bench press 325 pounds. Sure, he was useful whenever we needed to vacuum under the sofa, but his abysmal showings when matched up against high-powered Superhero strongmen stopped many a world-takeover attempt dead in its tracks.

Someone with wings

Whether providing advance scouting, swooping silently down from above to scoop up a hostage, or transporting you to safety when one of your schemes goes horribly wrong, one of these feathered felons would be a fabulous fit for your fiendish force. Unfortunately, all of the really good bird-based nicknames, like Hawkman and the Vulture, were taken years ago, and you may find yourself stuck with one of the newer guys like Hummingbirdman or the Tufted Titmouse.

Tip: These avian evildoers spend most of their free time perched on tree limbs or telephone wires, so you'll want to carry an umbrella when strolling around your lair grounds, especially right after lunch. And don't let them anywhere near your statues.

A super-intellectual

Not everyone is blessed with brainpower capable of reshaping a planet. In fact, I may be the only one. Yet even I enlisted the services of a super-intellectual to help with such complex tasks as programming the supercomputers, designing death rays, and uploading videos on to YouTube. This freed me up to issue more ultimatums.

This socially backward superdweeb is easily bullied yet also grateful for the opportunity to work in a well-equipped laboratory. This tends to make him an extremely loyal underling as well as a potential right-hand man.

What to look for: 90 percent of a super-intellectual's head should be located above his eyebrows and feature a clearly visible network of pulsating blood vessels. An exposed brain visible beneath a transparent dome is also acceptable. He should be small with a frail physique so that any energy he receives from food sources will be directed almost entirely to the brain.

Where to look for him: Radio Shack.

Tip: Always address your super-intellectual as "imbecile" or "dolt" no matter how much smarter he is than you. This will help keep his self-confidence low and will spare you the hassle of remembering his name.

An invisible being

When evil stealth is required, nothing can match the translucent tiptoeing of invisible Supervillains. Their ability to slink about undetected allows them to sneak into Superhero headquarters in order to attend secret meetings, gain access to classified documents, and hide the television remote. Of course, you, yourself, won't know where they are, either, which can lead to some awkward moments, particularly in the men's room. I made my own transparent underling, InvisiBill, wear a cowbell around his neck whenever he was in the lair.

Tip: Require all non-visible members of your team to report directly to you at the beginning and end of each day. These see-through scallywags are notorious for slipping in late and sneaking out early.

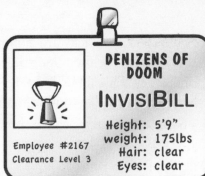

DENIZENS OF DOOM

INVISIBILL

Height: 5'9"
weight: 175lbs
Hair: clear
Eyes: clear

Employee #2167
Clearance Level 3

A shape-shifter

A shape-shifter's ability to imitate anyone on the planet is a wondrously wicked weapon when in the hands of a shrewd Supervillain who best knows how to use it. I, for example, once had my shape-shifter take on the appearance of David Beckham so we could get a discount on football shoes at my local sports shop. **MUHAHAHAHA!!**

They can also mimic Superheroes, allowing you to make those heroic ham bones look like complete wedgeheads in public. You can even have your shape-shifter take on *your* appearance so you can ~~run away~~ fall back and devise a new strategy when the going gets too dangerous. Of course, you will want to remain close enough so you can quickly jump back into the spotlight if any groveling occurs.

Someone who can control the weather

None of my evil plans ever called for weather control, per se, but I'll be a zombie's behind if I was ever going to let it rain on my birthday.

A fast guy

Superhuman speed is a power in very high demand among hopeful World Conquerors. A top-level speedster can outrace a bullet. He can disarm an entire regiment in the blink of an eye. He can commit a crime halfway around the globe and be back with a McDonald's faster than you can say, "Anything but McNuggets," and that includes bathroom breaks. You should look for a speed burner with a few years of experience under his belt, since it takes a while to get this particular power under complete control.

I once briefly employed a young man named Litespead who, along with being an extraordinarily poor speller, could run completely around the Earth in twelve seconds flat. Unfortunately, it took him a day and a half to come to a complete stop afterward, so I had no real use for him. Something else to be aware of—keeping these speed merchants in motion will cost you a bundle because they tend to burn through their boots at the costly rate of seven pairs/second.

Someone who looks like this

No superpowers necessary.

There are many other Supervillain
types roaming about in search of an evil
leader, many of whom might prove useful
to you. Pick and choose wisely, however—
just because a Supervillain possesses a
superpower doesn't make him a super
good fit for your lethal legion.

TWELFTH COMMANDMENT OF INCOMPREHENSIBILITY

Never bring a Supervillain into your organization who possesses
the power of invulnerability. There is nothing more frustrating than
trying to punish an underling who is impervious to harm.

SUPERHERO SPIES

The messiest situation you are likely to face when assembling your team (unless, that is, you ignore my warning and bring the Whizzer on board) involves accidentally bringing a Superhero spy into your midst. Once one of these deceitful do-gooders worms his way into your organization, it will be nearly impossible to flush him out before he causes serious damage. As you may recall, this very issue led to my leaving the Denizens of Doom (due to circumstances that were, as you may also recall, completely beyond my control). It also led to the creation of my unfailingly foolproof procedure to determine whether a Supervillain is, in actuality, a *Superhero* in disguise:

VORDAK THE INCOMPREHENSIBLE'S
Indescribable Undercover-Superhero Spy-Detection Procedure

Step 1.   Perform a visual check. Does he have perfect posture and a chin like a block of granite? If so, he may be a Superhero. Proceed to step 2.

Step 2.   Hand him an index card containing the phrase "In the name of truth and justice!" and have him read it aloud. Does his chest swell, his voice deepen, and his right index finger point upward involuntarily? If so, he may be a Superhero. Proceed to step 3.

Step 3. Have him advise a group of random elementary-school students to disrespect their elders and drop out of school the minute they turn sixteen years old. Does he collapse on to the floor and begin to shake violently? If so, he may be a Superhero. Proceed to step 4.

Step 4. Have him stand with his feet shoulder-width apart, fists resting on hips, and chin thrust slightly upward. Does a sudden breeze hit him head on, even while indoors? If so, he is definitely a Superhero. Bind him securely and drop him into one of your diabolically clever yet extremely slow-acting death traps.

I grant you permission to use my perfectly penned procedure as often as you please, as long as you refer to it aloud as "Vordak the Incomprehensible's Indescribable Undercover-Superhero Spy-Detection Procedure" at least three times whenever you use

This guy is definitely a Superhero.

it. This shouldn't be too difficult for anyone with half a brai . . .
On second thought, here is an example to follow:

"All right, [*insert Supervillain name here*], I just need to
run through Vordak the Incomprehensible's Indescribable
Undercover-Superhero Spy-Detection Procedure in order to
determine whether you are, in fact, a Superhero. Let's see now,
where did I put my copy of Vordak the Incomprehensible's
Indescribable Undercover-Superhero Spy-Detection Procedure?
Ah, yes. It's right here in the folder labeled 'Vordak the
Incomprehensible's Indescribable Undercover-Superhero
Spy-Detection Procedure'."

WORKING TOGETHER TOWARD A BETTER TOMORROW

Assuming you have enough sense to follow my advice to the
letter (doubtful, I know), you should have no problem putting
together a deadly organization capable of wreaking havoc on
humanity—so long as everyone works together toward that
goal. Dissension among the ranks will flush even the best-laid
plan down the toilet of self-destruction. So how can you keep
your underlings in line? By allowing them to have a say in what
is going on.

SUGGESTION BOX

Back in my Evil Masterminding days, whenever we gathered around the Conference Table of Gloom, I always made it a point to promote an atmosphere of openness and freedom. If anyone disagreed with me for any reason, that individual had the freedom to voice his or her opinion, while I had the freedom to pull a lever under the table that lowered his or her chair into a vat of molten titanium. This approach helped keep everyone on the same page—which is important because even *I* can't do *everything* myself.

By the way, congratulations are in order for your making it through this entire chapter without asking one stupid question.

"Thanks. So . . . does this mean we're buddies now?"

Scratch that.

If you were to approach me out of the blue and ask me what I miss most about being an active Supervillain, my response would be simple: I would staple a cheeseburger to your behind and toss you into a cage full of underfed badgers. I hate being approached out of the blue.

I do like the question, however, so I am going to give you a real treat by answering it. It's all the glorious stuff—the wonderfully evil gadgets, contraptions, weapons, and vehicles—that I miss the most. Well, that and the groveling. I really, really, really miss the groveling. Whether it came from a single henchman or the entire population of Rhode Island, it just gave me a warm, fuzzy feeling inside. Ah, yes, those were the days . . .

"Umm, excuse me, Your Incomprehensibleness?"

. . . kidnapped citizens begging for mercy . . .

"I believe you were going to tell us about all the neat stuff we get to use as Evil Supervillains."

. . . underlings licking my boots with hope of gaining my favor . . .

"Hey, look! It's COMMANDER VIRTUE!"

Huh? What? Where? I, uh . . . I'll be right back. I need to do some routine maintenance on my escape pod!

"No, wait! Come back! I was kidding. I just wanted to snap you out of that daydream you were in."

Oh. I see.

THIRTEENTH COMMANDMENT OF INCOMPREHENSIBILITY

Never, under any circumstances, are you to interrupt Vordak the Incomprehensible while he is daydreaming. For all you know, he could be in the middle of devising a diabolically sinister plan to take over the world, if not the entire galaxy.

(See Fourteenth Commandment)

FOURTEENTH COMMANDMENT OF INCOMPREHENSIBILITY

Unless he is about to be overwhelmed by an angry swarm of mutated harvester ants, in which case you should interrupt him *immediately*, using a frying pan if necessary.

Now that my breathing and heart rate have returned to normal, I shall continue. **DON'T EVER DO THAT AGAIN!** And do not read another syllable of this chapter until after you sit down and craft a two-thousand-word apology to me in which the phrase "I am a lousy, no-good eel dropping" appears at least seventeen times.

Now, where was I? Oh, yes—I was about to discuss all the wonderful devices that the serious Supervillain will have at his disposal. Let's begin by taking a look at . . .

DIABOLICALLY CLEVER YET EXTREMELY SLOW-ACTING DEATH TRAPS

Would it surprise you to learn that Supervillains have been using diabolically clever yet extremely slow-acting death traps on their enemies for tens of thousands of years?

"No."

Liar! Of course it would surprise you. From what I can tell, *any* basic piece of information would surprise you. You don't appear to be the brightest bulb in the chandelier, if you know what I'm saying.

"I don't."

Of course you don't. After all, you don't seem to be the sharpest arrow in the quiver, if you catch my drift.

"I don't."

Of course you don't. After all, you aren't exactly the ... the pointiest ... thingy ... ACK! Your dimwittedness is tying my brain in knots! Although, on the bright side, at least your sentences have gotten shorter. Whether it surprises you or *not*, death traps have been around for thousands of years. Just take a look at this primitive cave painting that was recently discovered in northern Spain:

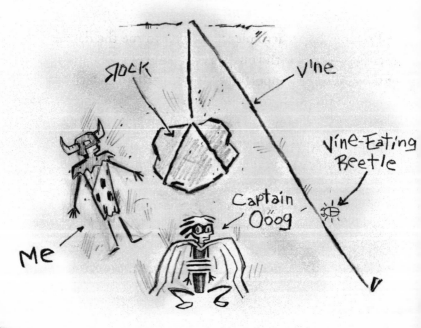

Yes, I was as shocked as you are to discover that primitive evildoers knew how to spell. It appears that we Supervillains have always been vastly more intelligent than the typical human being—at least until you joined our ranks. So, what is it about these tantalizingly treacherous traps that have made them so popular among Supervillains for so many years? To answer this question, we need to closely examine:

VORDAK THE INCOMPREHENSIBLE'S
Un-Do-Withoutable List of the Positives and Negatives of Using Diabolically Clever Yet Extremely Slow-Acting Death Traps

Positives

- Provides Superhero plenty of time to rue the day he crossed paths with you.
- Creates ample opportunity for Superhero to beg you for mercy (although, to be honest, the only Superhero to ever beg me for mercy was the Baffling Beggar, and that was pretty much all he ever did, anyway).
- Allows you to reveal the details of your sinister plan, per Regulation 7.1b (see page 89).
- Allows you to remind the Superhero over and over and over and over how foolish he was to believe he could defeat you.
- Gives you a chance to use the restroom.

Negatives

- Never, ever, even once in recorded history, has a Superhero failed to escape before he has been harmed.

"Excuse me again, Your Humongousness. I may be off base here, but it kind of seems like that one negative pretty much outweighs the positives. Why not just dispose of him quickly and be done with it? That's what I would do."

Well, I guess that's why you are the piddling banana slug in this relationship and I am the incomprehensibly evil Super Genius. Sure, it would be a fairly simple matter to sneak up behind your arch-nemesis and zap him with a ray that transforms him into a block of granite. Sure, you could then drop him into the ocean and he would sink to the bottom like a stone (or a block of granite), never to be heard from again. Sure, this would make your conquest of the planet a whole lot easier. But do you know what? Your arch-nemesis would meet his demise without ever knowing *who* did him in. And where, I ask you, is the joy in that? No, a *real* Supervillain will always opt for the diabolically clever yet extremely slow-acting death trap, no matter how small the odds of success. Heck, Commander Virtue narrowly escaped the clutches of my own diabolical death traps thirty-seven* times, but that never stopped me from throwing him into another one.

---

* THIRTY-EIGHT, IF YOU COUNT THE TIME HE ESCAPED MY CRUSHING-WALLS-OF-DOOM ROOM, THEN ALLOWED HIMSELF TO BE RECAPTURED AND ESCAPED AGAIN JUST TO RUB IT IN.

Now, I should make myself clear on something. When I say "slow-acting" death trap, I don't mean too slow. You are looking to fill your arch-nemesis with a sense of dread, not boredom. If he becomes weary of the whole process, he is likely to beg you just to go ahead and finish him off, in which case you have to let him go. You must always do the opposite of what someone begs you to do. It's the Supervillain way. Unfortunately, Commander Virtue figured this out and now uses it to his advantage. ("No, Vordak! I beg of you! Don't set your laser pistol on the floor and then knock yourself unconscious with that steel pipe!")

This death trap is *too* slow-acting.

There are three main types of diabolical death traps that have remained popular over the years and that I, myself, have used many times. All are guaranteed to come extremely close to exterminating your captured arch-nemesis. You are welcome to construct one or more of these in your own lair or, if you think you can do better *(Give me a moment, here. I'm laughing so hard I'm snorting diabolical snot all over my keyboard!)*, feel free to design something of your own *(snort)*.

FIFTEENTH COMMANDMENT OF INCOMPREHENSIBILITY

Never include a countdown timer when designing your diabolically clever yet extremely slow-acting death traps. Although they can be extremely slow-acting, they aren't all that diabolically clever.

Trap #1. Slowly Being Lowered to Ultimate Doom

This particular trap requires that you bind your Superhero securely with a rope or cable and then lower him slowly into something horrifyingly fatal. You have the option of dropping him down headfirst, but this will give you less time to enjoy his screams of agony. This is the trap of choice when a sidekick has been captured along with his mentor.

Popular Method of Escape: The hero (or heroes) swing rhythmically back and forth and then uses a knife from his utility belt to cut through his bindings and drop clear of danger.

Most common forms of this trap (in increasing order of cruelty):

Boiling Lava

Bloodthirsty Piranhas

Sulfuric Acid

Maria's 6th Birthday Party

Trap #2. Moving Slowly Along a Conveyor Belt Toward Ultimate Doom

This is an outstanding death trap for the Supervillain who has limited ceiling height in his lair. Simply tie your victim to the conveyor belt, set the speed, and gaze gleefully as he gradually glides toward his grisly goodbye. This adversary assassination apparatus does tend to be a bit noisy, so you will need to speak up when taunting your fallen foe.

Popular Method of Escape: A sidekick, girlfriend, or some other conniving cohort shows up at the last second and pulls the conveniently labeled power lever to the Off position.

Most common forms of this trap (in increasing order of fiendishness):

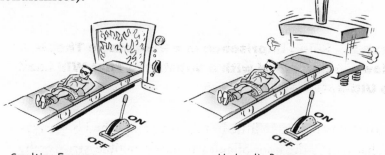

Smelting Furnace

Hydraulic Press

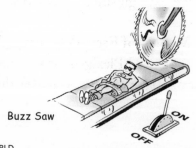

Buzz Saw

Never-Ending, Brain-Melting
Theme Park Ride

Trap #3. Being Imprisoned in a Receptacle That Is Slowly Being Filled with a Substance That Will Lead to Ultimate Doom

In this abominable little beauty, the vanquished Superhero is shackled to the floor of a nearly indestructible, structurally enhanced Plexiglas tank, which is then slowly filled with any number of life-extinguishing substances.

Popular Method of Escape: Nearly indestructible, structurally enhanced Plexiglas tank is shattered by falling debris resulting from an unexpected earthquake.

Most common forms of this trap (in increasing order of downright not-niceness):

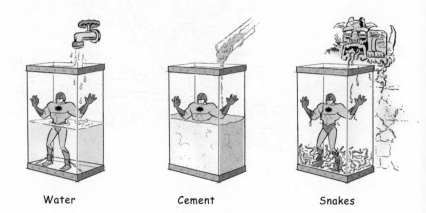

Water

Cement

Snakes

Larry Krabbenhoft

BAKED BEANS

VILLAINOUS VEHICLES

As you go about your business of conquering the planet, you will find it necessary to leave the comfortable confines of your lair from time to time. There will be armies to lead, nations to conquer, and garbage cans to take to the curb. And when you head out, you will want to do so with a style that proclaims to the world "I am POWERFUL and EVIL and BETTER THAN YOU!" You have worked hard to create a sinister image for yourself, and you don't want to blow it by tooling around town in a mini-van.

I, myself, have always had a certain flair when it comes to abominable buggies. I dug back into my photo album and grabbed a few examples:

Here I am at eighteen months, playing with the family cat while snuggled securely in my wonderfully wicked walker. Am I adorable, or what? Normally, I would have been at Junior Gym Jamboree, but the instructor sent me home because I "did not play well with others". Mom and Dad were very proud.

I got this little beauty for my tenth birthday. Dad customized it with a miniaturized Pratt & Whitney JT12 Turbojet engine. I could run through my entire paper route in 13.7 seconds, although it probably would have taken a bit longer had I actually delivered the papers. I named this terrifying transport the Roscoenator, in honor of my pet hamster, Roscoe. That's him on the handlebars.

My job at Burger Dictator gave me enough money to buy and customize a horrifically heinous hot rod when I was nineteen. Here I am on my way to work to discuss my performance review with my supervisor.

Chances are, you will also have need of other, more specialized vehicles. After all, that tunnel from your lair to Fort Knox isn't going to dig itself. Depending on the type of evil plans you devise, you will require vehicles that travel on water and through the air. You will require vehicles that travel over mountains and across deserts. You will require vehicles that travel to the bottom of the ocean and beneath the Earth's crust.

You will require a very large garage.

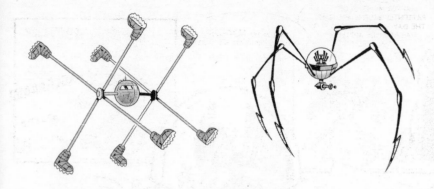

Lastly, we have the enormous, weaponized vehicles. These tyrannical transports not only get you where you want to go, but they let you dish out a little destruction along the way. When you are ready to reveal yourself to the world, this is an excellent way to do it. In order to impress the TV news networks and receive maximum worldwide coverage, focus on destroying targets that will cause dramatic explosions, like an oil refinery or a gunpowder-storage facility or the bathroom in Harlan Pluggedbowel's apartment.

Harlan Pluggedbowel

WEAPONS

No chapter on evil goodies would be complete without a section on weapons. I'm not talking about laser pistols and dynamite and the other minor things—we will cover those later. I'm talking about the big stuff, the glorious high-end Superweapons that you will use to bring the planet's inhabitants to their knees. I'm talking about machines of mayhem such as:

- *Tractor beams*
- *Global-weather disruptors*
- *Molecular destabilizers*
- *Planetary-water evaporators*
- *Vortex generators*
- *Oxygen destroyers*
- *Earth-core superheaters*

- *Disintegration rays*
- *Mind-control rays*
- *Heat rays / Freeze rays*
- *Shrink rays*
- *Growth rays*
- *Death rays*
- *Lasers*

These are the tools that will make
your evil plans hum, the instruments
with which you will threaten to shake
the planet to its very core. And you
certainly are not limited to this list.
Your super-intellectual, the geeky little
toad that he is, will be thrilled to help
you create any type of specialized
Superweapon you desire. It's what gets him
out of bed in the morning . . . well, that and the fear that he
will be thrown into a vat of radioactive waste if he sleeps in
past 6:00 a.m.

You are no doubt soiling your trousers in excitement just
thinking about the possibilities that lie before you, weapon-wise.
You may even be tempted to begin work on four or five or
even more different Superweapons right off the bat, but
I would advise against it. Choose one and build it to
perfection. That way you will become known as "the Heat-
Ray Guy" or "the Vortex-Generator Guy" or what have you,
which will only add to your villainous vibe.

A Word of Caution: Because the Earth, like many planets, is round, it may be necessary to bounce your beam or ray off a satellite in order to hit your desired target. This requires precise aim and can be very tricky, especially for a spaz such as yourself. Because I am as generous as I am Incomprehensible, I have created this handy reference card to help you out. Photocopy it, laminate it, and keep it pinned to your utility belt at all times.

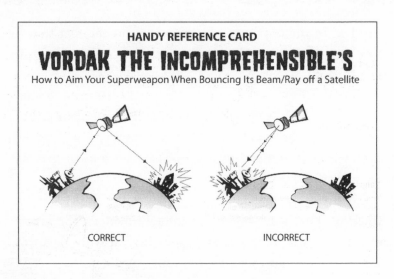

ODDS AND ENDS OF EVIL

Of course, not all of your evil activities will require the type of major hardware we have been talking about. You and your super-intellectual will have your hands full designing and building your various death traps, vehicles, and Superweapons, so for the day-to-day evil necessities, I suggest using an evil mail-order retailer such as Sinister Syd.

11

CHAPTER SEVEN
The EVIL Plan

Vordak's TO DO List
- ~~pick up cape from cleaners~~
- ~~feed dog~~
- ~~wash and wax Spiderbot~~
- ~~get haircut~~
- rule the world
- MUAHAHAHAHA!!

In previous chapters I have ~~wasted~~ spent a great deal of my valuable time arming you with the tools necessary to vanquish this spitball of a planet. I trust you were paying attention.

"I'm sorry—what was that?"

I said, "I TRUST YOU WERE PAYING ATTENTION!"

"Oh, yeah! Definitely!"

Excellent! So, with all that awesome might at your command, you're probably thinking you'll just relax in the comfort of your evil lair and wait for the world to surrender. Well, guess what? I've already tried that. The only ones who surrendered to me were sixteen seventh-grade students from Lester P. Grace Middle School, and they did so only to avoid taking Mr. Crapdavitch's third-period algebra exam. So what is the lesson, here?

"Try to get Miss Mosquera for algebra?"

Exactly. She lets you use a calculator and keeps a big jar of Milk Duds on the . . . I MEAN, NO! My point is that if you intend to rule more than sixteen seventh-grade slackers, you will need to get up off your duff and put together a plan. A plan that is evil. An EVIL PLAN.

THE EVIL PLAN

There are evil plans, and then there are EVIL PLANS. Let's say you want to embarrass your older brother by drawing streaks in his underwear using a brown Magic Marker. When will you strike? How will you deflect the blame on to your little sister? What will you use to disinfect your hands afterward? These are the sorts of issues that are covered in an evil plan. Other examples of evil plans include schemes to toilet paper your principal's house (did it), switch the signs on toilet doors (did it), and spray water on the front of Jimmy Licata's cargo shorts so everyone thinks he has had an "accident" (planning it as we speak). Yes, they are plans and, yes, they are evil, but they are limited in their size and scope.

Now, truly EVIL PLANS, the kind with all upper case letters, come in three basic types (listed in increasing order of evilosity):

1. Those designed to conquer the world.
2. Those designed to destroy the world.
3. Those designed to trick you into eating cauliflower.

Obviously, based on the title of this book, I prefer type 1.

"Wait a minute. So you're telling me there are other Supervillains out there creating EVIL PLANS type 2 and 3 who are more evil than you?"

HA!! Hardly! Don't confuse the *plan* with the *person*. Yes, destroying the world would be the more evil thing to do. But here is the problem: no world = no people. No people = no groveling. No groveling = no joy for Vordak the Incomprehensible. Besides, if you were to destroy the world, what then? Where would you live? What would you do? Whom would you torment? Conquering and ruling are really the only sensible things to do, but if you are dead set on *destroying* the world, I would highly recommend this book:

HOW TO DESTROY The Earth and Other Terrestrial Planets!

By Doctor Destructo

Doctor Destructo is very well respected among evil masterminds, and his other books, *How to Destroy Jupiter and Other Gas Giants* and *An Idiot's Guide to Imploding the Universe* are best-sellers within the Supervillain community.

WARNING!—Have plenty of tissues on hand before reading the next paragraph.

Okay, now it's time to brace yourself for a bit of bad news. When it comes to designing the details of your own EVIL PLAN, I am afraid I cannot help you. I know, I know. This must come as a huge disappointment to you, and I certainly don't blame you for bawling your eyes out. After all, it is I, Vordak the Incomprehensible, whose help you will not be receiving. But a truly sinister, fiendishly diabolical EVIL PLAN can be carried out only by the individual whose twisted imagination came up with it in the first place. And no two EVIL PLANS are exactly alike because no two EVIL SUPERVILLAINS are alike. Take you and me, for example. I have a brilliant mind, a wondrous wit, and striking good looks, while you approximate a bullfrog in each of these areas. Nevertheless, I have spent the better part of seven chapters giving you all the tools and knowledge you will need to prepare your own EVIL PLAN, so get cracking.

"I can't think of anything."

Wow . . . what a surprise. Let's see if we can kick-start that "brain" of yours and get you in a plan-devising mood with a little mental exercise.

Help Vordak the Incomprehensible snatch the beryllium energy sphere from its protective vault deep within the confines of the top secret, high-security government facility. You have two seconds. BEGIN! *(Solution on next page.)*

Solution:

Simple! For me, that is. As you can see, the words *fair play* are not in my vocabulary. Well, they are in my vocabulary, but only to say that they aren't.

All right, now that your brain is warmed up and ready to go, you should have no trouble devising a truly inspired, utterly brilliant EVIL PLAN. I believe in you! *(Oh, man. Hold on a second. Now I'm laughing so hard I just spit milk all over the diabolical snot that was already on my keyboard!)*

What Can Go Wrong?

If your EVIL PLAN is not successful, it will be for one of the following reasons:

> REASON #1: Something unexpected happens. This one is pretty straightforward. Let's face it, if you mastermind a plan that is foiled by something you *expected* to happen, then you must have cabbage for brains.

> REASON #2: You have cabbage for brains.

Unfortunately, there is not much you can do about either of these.

"What about Superheroes?"

They fall under Reason #1. Although it's true that you can pretty much *expect* your arch-nemesis to swoop in and thwart your EVIL PLAN, how and when he does so will be completely *unexpected*. I can't begin to recount the number of times I have come painfully close to seeing an EVIL PLAN reach fruition only to have that leotard-laden lackwit Commander Virtue gum up the works—including the time he destroyed my Atmosphere Disintegrator by literally throwing a wad of gum into it.

Here are a few EVIL PLANS from my own files that were not successful. I am allowing you to view them so you can see that these brilliant schemes failed through no fault of my own. And, who knows—you might even learn something. *(Zounds! There I go again. My gut is killing me, here!)*

Diabolical EVIL PLAN 47a

Summary: Send my entire minion army of robots, clones, and zombies on a mission to overthrow Disney World. Once world leaders see how easily I can take away humanity's greatest pleasures, they will turn control of the planet over to me immediately.

Required: 20,000–30,000 minions (various types)
$2 million–$3 million (for park entrance fees)
300 gallons of sunscreen
Result: Not good
Reason: I underestimated how much my minion army would enjoy Space Mountain

3,550 MIN WAIT FROM THIS POINT

Diabolical EVIL PLAN 117b:

Summary: In light of the failure of EVIL PLAN 117a (using shrink ray to reduce entire world population to an average height of 3 ½ inches), EVIL PLAN 117b will achieve the same overall effect with less effort by reversing the ray and transforming myself into a hundred-foot-tall colossus. I will then rampage across the countryside, terrifying the populace and leaving untold destruction in my wake. Horrified world leaders will turn control of the planet over to me immediately.

Required: Growth ray

Comfortable walking shoes

A 400-pound bag of trail mix (for snack breaks while rampaging)

Result: Not good

Reason: I didn't realize that the ray had no effect on metal. I ended up with a screaming headache and couldn't get my helmet off for a month.

Diabolical EVIL PLAN 12a:

Summary: Definitely one of my more ambitious EVIL PLANS. Using my ingenious Vorcuum Siphoning Device, I will suck all the water from the Earth's oceans. When world leaders discover they no longer have anywhere to put their ships, they will turn control of the planet over to me immediately.

Required: Vorcuum Siphoning Device
Spare battery
Containers to store water
Map pinpointing locations of oceans
Result: Not good
Reason: That portly purveyor of justice, the Masked Manatee, unwittingly swam too close to the suction nozzle

THE ULTIMATUM

When your plan is ready and you have all the pieces in place, you need to alert the world to your evil intentions. You do this by issuing an *ultimatum*.

An ultimatum should contain the following basic information:

- Who you are.
- Who you are threatening.
- What you are threatening to do.
- What your demands are.
- How much time those you are threatening have to meet these demands.

"That sounds easy enough, but I can't shake the feeling that there are four or five common mistakes to avoid when issuing ultimatums."

HAH!! There are *six*!

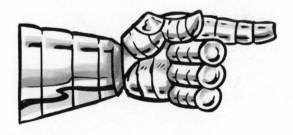

VORDAK THE INCOMPREHENSIBLE'S

Six Mistakes to Avoid When Issuing Ultimatums

Mistake #1. Using language that you do not understand

Since you have no doubt been dazzled by my own voluminous vocabulary, you may be tempted to try to impress your fellow Earth dwellers by using important-sounding words in your ultimatums. While this is not a problem for a supergenius such as myself, it likely *is* a problem for *you*, since you have thus far demonstrated the brainpower of a glazed doughnut. To save you from embarrassing yourself, I have included a little exercise to test your villainous vocabulary:

You wish to intimidate the president of Uborkistan. Which threat would you choose in each of the following examples?

1.
(A) "I will agglutinate your decranons!"
(B) "I will fimbriate your dungarees!"

2.
(A) "I will meliorate your lineaments!"
(B) "I will gormandize your *Phodopus sungorus*!"

3.
(A) "I will purloin your chattels!"
(B) "I will osculate your phalanges!"

4.

(A) "I will exfoliate your epidermis!"

(B) "I will geniculate your jejunum!"

5.

(A) "I will burnish your balmorals!"

(B) "I will conglobate your progeny!"

Translations (more sinister threat in bold)

1.

(A) You are threatening to glue his elbows together.

(B) You are offering to hem his jeans.

2.

(A) You are offering to improve the look of his face.

(B) You are threatening to wolf down his Winter White Russian dwarf hamster.

3.

(A) You are threatening to steal his personal belongings

(B) You are offering to kiss his toes.

4.

(A) You are offering to gently remove his old, dead skin
   cells, giving him a more healthy and youthful
   appearance.

**(B) You are threatening to tie his small intestine in
   knots.**

5.

(A) You are offering to polish his boots.

**(B) You are threatening to gather up all of his children
   and form them into a giant ball.**

If you failed to choose the more sinister threat in *any* of the
five examples above, you are better off filling your ultimatums
with words you can understand, like *it* and *is* and, if you're
really feeling like a smarty-pants, *the*.

Mistake #2. Making spelling errors

This can be a real problem with written or electronically submitted threats. You may spend weeks working on your ultimatum, tweaking and polishing it to diabolical perfection, but it won't matter if no one knows what you are talking about. Mis-spelling even one word—for example, *laser*—can seriously take the oomph out of an otherwise spectacular ultimatum.

"... and if you fail to give me complete control of the planet within the next twelve hours, I will have no choice but to unleash the *world's biggest LOSER!*"

Mistake #3. Making translation errors

Issuing ultimatums to the leaders of foreign countries can be tricky. Years ago, I decided to threaten the chancellor of Germany with a plague of foul-smelling frogs if he did not deliver twenty tons of gold bullion to me within forty-eight hours. At the time, one of my underlings was Kommandant Kaboom, a sinister German explosives expert. He performed the translation, and I sent the chancellor the following message:

Ich habe Kröten in beiden Ohren. Schauen Sie bitte in meinen Nasenlöchern.

Which, as it turns out, means ...

I have toads in both ears. Please look in my nostrils.

It was only after I transmitted the ultimatum that I discovered the good kommandant's brain had been reduced to tapioca pudding as a result of repeated exposure to his explosive blasts

Mistake #4. Targeting the wrong individual

Threatening to bury the entire state of New Mexico under a twelve-foot layer of expired cottage cheese unless you receive $100 billion may seem like a brilliantly clever ultimatum, but not if you issue it to an asparagus farmer in Ohio. Sure, he doesn't want to see his fellow countrymen suffer, but what are you going to do with $100 billion worth of asparagus? Make sure that the individuals you target are in positions of power, and, no, just because Zack and Cody are on six times a day does not mean they direct world policy.

Mistake #5. Failing to maintain the position of power

You have issued your ultimatum in truly sinister fashion. World leaders are terrified and ready to meet your every demand. Be careful not to do anything stupid that would give your adversaries the upper hand.

Mistake #6. **Coming across as unprofessional**

If you are delivering your ultimatum in person, via video, or by hijacking the world's television airwaves, it is important to present a positive image if you hope to be taken seriously. Your costume should be clean with no wrinkles, and any armor should be polished and dent free. If you sport a sinister mustache and/or beard, make sure they are neatly trimmed and have all the potato chip crumbs vacuumed out. Your posture, whether sitting or standing, should be upright and attentive. Your teeth should be brushed and flossed, and your hair, if exposed, should be neatly shaped and styled. And be sure to memorize your ultimatum and practice it repeatedly until you have it down pat. If you have a high, squeaky voice, you might consider installing a voice synthesizer beneath your helmet or mask. Avoid the frequent use of "ums" and "ahs" and "you knows", and just generally try to avoid sounding like a professional athlete.

Now it's your turn to give it a shot. Write your own practice ultimatum and send it to me immediately so that I may review it.

Well, it's about time! Let's take a look. Hmmm ... I am actually quite impressed by this—if a mountain goat wrote it. Otherwise, this is an *extremely* weak effort. Let me just go ahead and mark this up with a few "suggestions":

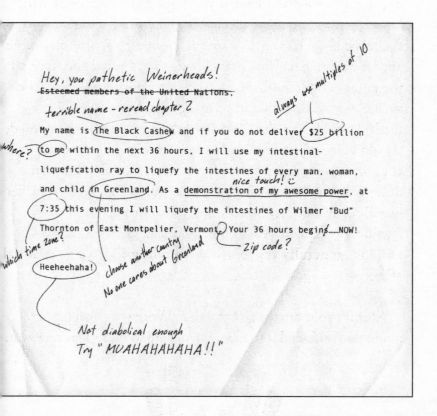

Now we're talking! And, although it pains me deeply, I must give you credit for coming up with the intestinal-liquefication ray. Perhaps I have been wrong about you. Perhaps you *do* have some promise after all.

"Oh, yeah!"

"You know it!"

"I'm awesome!"

"That's me!"

"Oh, yeah!"

"You know it!"

"I'm awesome!"

"That's me!"

Ack.

CHAPTER EIGHT
Congratulations, You Rule the World! Now What?

Just between us, I always knew that it would be you, whatever your name is, who would use my brilliantly evil advice to conquer the planet. All the other potato heads who bought this book never had a chance, did they? Those poor, pathetic little mudworms. All that time spent designing their costumes, gathering their minions, creating their lairs and weapons, issuing their ultimatums—and for what? Absolutely nothing, that's what. You beat them to the punch and now they, like everyone else on this miserable little planet, must bow to your diabolical magnificence. MUAHAHAHAHA!!

"Uh . . . excuse me, Your Reprehensibleness, but I haven't actually conquered the planet yet."

You haven't? Then why in Zolnar's name are you reading this? Did you not see the plainly worded warning above this chapter's title? It's pretty hard to miss, what with the large letters and the big box around it. Am I to understand that you are unable to follow even the *simplest* instruc

Note to publisher: Be sure to place this warning at the beginning of chapter 8.

— Vordak

WARNING!

DO NOT READ THIS CHAPTER UNTIL YOU BECOME THE ACTUAL RULER OF THE WORLD!

Ack!! This is what happens when you rely on simpletons to help publish your book! Rest assured that I will hunt down the blundering buffoon responsible for this egregious gaffe, and let's just say he or she will not have the opportunity to make another mistake—*ever again*! In the meantime, if you *have* conquered the world, continue reading. If you *have not,* then ignore that first paragraph, get back out there, follow my advice, keep trying, you can do it, blah, blah, blah. Come back to this chapter after you conquer the world.

Okay, all those miserable little failures are gone. Now, where were we? Ah, yes—congratulations on becoming the **Evil Ruler of the World!** The glorious gift of my guidance has made all that you have accomplished possible. The entire planet, and everything on it, is now yours to command. You are free to do whatever you please, whenever you choose, to whomever you want. And, what's even *more* exciting, you now qualify to receive your very own official Certificate of Completion! Simply send me proof of your worldwide rulership in the form of $500 billion worth of gold bullion delivered to my doorstep, and your certificate will be in the mail the next day!

Vordak the Incomprehensible's

EVIL RULER OF THE WORLD
Certificate of Completion

Is hereby granted to

Malzor The Unmercifully Heartless

for successfully completing his training and achieving the glorious status of EVIL RULER OF THE WORLD! He realizes that his conquering of the Earth was made possible only through the teachings and advice of VORDAK THE INCOMPREHENSIBLE, whom he believes to be the most brilliantly evil, not to mention best-looking, individual who ever walked the face of this or any other planet.

Vordak the Incomprehensible

Vordak the Incomprehensible
Diabolical Mastermind/Evil Genius

So, Mr. Planetary Boss Man, Mr. Fancy Pants, Mr. Big Cheese—now that the entire world is your personal plaything, what are you going to do first?

"I'm not sure. I was thinking maybe I would sink Hawaii or go see a movie or something."

GREAT GASSY GOBLINS! Will my instruction never cease? You need to be *creative* in your torment or risk losing the respect of humanity! All right, here is what I am going to do. I am going to give you one final list. This is strictly a freebie from me to you—the information you paid for ended seven sentences ago. This list contains things that I, myself, was planning to do if I ever became the **RULER OF THE WORLD!** Some are sensationally sinister, while others are merely cunningly clever. But all come directly from the magnificent mind of Vordak the Incomprehensible!

VORDAK THE INCOMPREHENSIBLE'S
Loathsome List of Things to Do Once You Become the Ruler of the World!

- **Decree** that all toys and electronics are to be packaged in impossible-to-open plastic shells. **MUAHAHAHAHA!!**

"Umm, the toy companies already do that, Your Despicableness."

What?! The world has become a more evil place than I even imagined! It appears I need to take my loathsome list up a fiendish notch or two.

- **Change iTunes to iTune** and make the only song available to download "I'm the Map!" from *Dora the Explorer*.

- **Destroy old holidays**. Holidays are joyful occasions when families and friends gather to celebrate important people or events from their history. Eliminate them all as quickly as possible, with the exception of Leif Eriksson Day (October 9). What can I say? I am a big fan of Vikings.

- **Create *new* holidays.** With Christmas, Easter, New Year's Day, Independence Day, National Sea Otter Awareness Week, and other holidays out of the picture, there are plenty of open calendar dates available to celebrate things of greater importance, namely ~~me~~ you. Hold weekly parades in your honor so that all may bask in the splendor of your magnificent majesty . . . or the magnificence of your majestic splendor . . . or, if you're really special, the majesty of your splendiferous magnificence.

• **Play "Being" Bowling.**

Have all the residents of a particular town line up in a
triangular shape and see how many you can knock down using
an enormous bowling ball. Start off with a small town such
as Mauckport, Indiana (population: 83), and, as your game
improves, move on to larger cities like Grank Pass, Oregon
(23,670), Gilbert, Arizona (109,697), and London, England
(7,172,091—you will need a very large ball for this one).

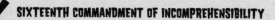

SIXTEENTH COMMANDMENT OF INCOMPREHENSIBILITY

When Being Bowling, always place the chubbier residents toward the front of the triangle for greater pin action.

- **Erect unimaginably humongous statues of yourself.**
Locate them so at least one is visible at all times from anywhere on Earth. These will serve as a constant reminder to the planet's pitiful population that you possess a preponderance of petrifyingly prodigious power.

• Create new words . . .

. . . such as the verb form of *Vordak* (always capitalized),
which means: "to apply a whooping of epic proportions."

Examples:
- Did you see the Steelers *Vordak* the Lions 63–0?
- Jason couldn't sit down for a week after his mom *Vordaked*
  him for putting bolognese sauce in the DVD player.

. . . or the adjective *Vordakian* (always capitalized), which
means: "(1) of unimaginable magnificence and/or splendor
or (2) of immeasurable evil."

Examples:
- The sunrise on Mercury is absolutely *Vordakian*.
- Brad's *Vordakian mother* wouldn't let him stay up to watch
  The X Factor.

• Play Diabolical Darts. For some completely
random destructive fun, blindfold yourself
and throw a dart at a map of the world. Then
launch a twenty-two-thousand-pound
D-3714 SuperDart programmed to land in
the exact same spot on the actual Earth.

- **Genetically alter the Earth's animal population.** There are over fifty thousand species of animals on the planet, and that doesn't even include insects. That's an awful lot of poop plopping down on to *your* planet's surface every single day. It's dirty, smelly, and, quite frankly, downright disrespectful. Combining animals will help minimize the problem. It also means zoos can be downsized to three or four cages, leaving you additional space to erect enormous statues of yourself.

DO NOT FEED THE MOOLEOPARKFLYDERCAMUCKISH

By the way, I *love* bacon cheeseburgers so, while you're at it . . .

• **Alter the planet's surface in tribute to yourself**. Supply every man, woman, and child on Earth with a shovel, pick, or hoe and have them reshape North America in your likeness. Not only will this pay lasting homage to your magnificence, it will also serve as a warning to beings from distant solar systems that you have already laid claim to this putrid little planet.

- **Create an anthem honoring your greatness** that the entire population of the planet must chant in unison three times a day. I wrote the lyrics to my own anthem a number of years ago, although I am still working on the melody:

ALL HAIL MIGHTY VORDAK!!

All hail mighty Vordak
The In-com-pre-hen-si-ble
Who can devastate a planet
With a simple lever pull.

His evil's overwhelming
His mercy, nonexistent
His awesomeness is legend
His costume—stain resistant.

He is smart and strong and mighty
And he's been that way since birth
He is truly awe-inspiring
The most handsome man on Earth.

I do not deserve to serve him
I'm but worthless, putrid scum
He's a wondrous, special being
I'm a paramecium.

If he commands me "Dig a ditch!"
I will quickly grab a shovel
If he passes through my village
I'll get on my knees and grovel.

So all hail mighty Vordak
In whose name I sweat and toil
For if I fail to please him
I'll be dipped in boiling oil.

- **Change the standard work week**. Have all planetary citizens between the ages of three and ninety-three work twenty-four hours a day, seven days a week, fifty-two weeks a year (with, of course, three five-minute breaks per day to chant my, er *your*, anthem). Those over the age of ninety-three get Sunday mornings between 8:30 and 8:45 off to disinfect their dentures.

Note: Although this is a wonderful idea, implementing it means you will not be able to do some of the other things I suggest because everyone will be busy working all the time.

- **Require every male junior high school geometry teacher over the age of forty to wear a tutu and ballet slippers**.

- **Work on perfecting a time machine**. Sure, tormenting those toiling under your iron-fisted rule can help make the days go by faster, but eventually you will need to find new challenges or you run the risk of becoming bored and, dare I say it, *less evil*. Perfecting a time machine will allow you to travel throughout the ages and reconquer the Earth in different eras in order to keep yourself sharp.

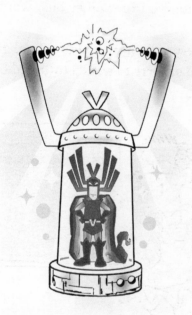

The key word here is *perfecting*. Be sure to thoroughly test your time machine on your henchmen before using it yourself. Otherwise, who knows when or where you might end up.

Bad Times and Places for Your Time Machine to Appear

January 3, 53,217 B.C.

May 19, 1963

April 15, 1912

August 7, 4291

Oh, and one last thing . . .

I'll bet you thought I forgot about our little agreement from way back on page 14. Needless to say, I will be seeing you soon . . . and I won't be packing light.
MUAHAHAHAHA!!

ABOUT THE AUTHOR

VORDAK THE INCOMPREHENSIBLE is a world-class Supervillain and the Evil Master of all he surveys. His previous writing includes his half of witty repartee with various Superheroes as well as numerous ultimatums to world leaders. This is his first book. His future projects include an autobiography titled *A Life Vastly Superior to Yours* as well as rewriting the literary classics *War and Peace* and *The Grapes of Wrath* in order to "make them better". His current whereabouts are unknown, where he is enjoying semi-retirement with his genetically altered dog, Armageddon. His presence has been unleashed into an unsuspecting Internet at www.vordak.com.

About the Minions

SCOTT SEEGERT was selected to transcribe Vordak's notes based on his ability to be easily captured. He has completely forgotten what fresh air smells like and has learned to subsist on a diet of beetles, shackle rust, and scabs. He hasn't brushed his teeth in over seventeen months. As far as he knows, he still has a wife and three children living in south-east Michigan.

JOHN MARTIN had the great misfortune of being chosen by Vordak to illustrate this book. He hasn't seen the sun in three years and spends his free time counting down the months to his annual change of underwear. He is deathly afraid of the dark and spiders, which is unfortunate considering his situation. The last he heard, he also had a wife and three children living in south-east Michigan.

EVIL NOTES:

Don't even _think_ about writing on these pages!
— Vordak